Claim your FREE
5:2 daily meal plans
to accompany this book!

5:2 DIET PHOTOS

600 food photos, 30 snack ideas & 60 great-tasting low-calorie recipes

1ST EDITION

First published in Great Britain in 2015
by Chello Publishing Limited
Registered Company Number 7237986
www.chellopublishing.co.uk | info@chellopublishing.co.uk

The information contained in this book is not a substitute for medical or other professional guidance. Please consult your GP before making any alterations to medications or changing medical treatment. Although all reasonable care has been taken in the writing of this book, the authors and publisher are not responsible for any specific health needs; they do not accept any legal responsibility or liability for any personal injury or other consequences, damage or loss arising from any use of information and advice contained within this book.

The authors have asserted their moral rights.

ISBN: 978-1-908261-09-0   Printed in the UK 1015

Authors	Chris Cheyette BSc (Hons) MSc RD
	Yello Balolia BA (Hons)
Text	Vanessa Quarmby BSc (Hons) MBDA RD
Photography	Yello Balolia BA (Hons)
Design & Layout	Lesley Mitchell
	Yello Balolia BA (Hons)
Cover Design	George Malache
Chef	Nicholas Witt

For more information, please visit:

www.carbsandcals.com

Contents

Introduction

Food can be an enriching part of life, though for many of us maintaining a balanced diet and healthy weight can be a constant challenge. Even if you only occasionally surf the internet, read a newspaper or pick up a magazine, you will notice many features on weight loss. There have been hundreds of weight loss books and plans over the years, but recently one has emerged that seems to be particularly effective for people who have struggled with other methods. The 5:2 approach enables you to lose weight without constant deprivation. Eating a normal, healthy diet 5 days a week, and fasting on the 2 remaining days, reduces your overall calorie intake and has proven to be an effective method for many people.

5:2 **Diet Photos** shows you visually how to implement the 5:2 fasting diet (also known as intermittent fasting), making it easier to choose foods on your 2 low-calorie fasting days. With 600 photos, 60 recipes and 30 snack ideas, this book will give you inspiration for great-tasting and easy-to-prepare meals and snacks to include on your 2 fasting days. It is designed as a support tool to complement the 5:2 diet, whether you have just started the regime, or have been following it for a while and are now struggling for new ideas on your fast days.

How does the 5:2 diet work?

A recent analysis of many weight loss studies concluded that overall calorie reduction is the most important factor in weight loss, rather than the actual composition of the diet. The 5:2 diet reduces your weekly calorie intake by 25%, while requiring you to diet for only 2 days a week. You eat normally for 5 days and fast on the other 2 days.

The main advantage of the 5:2 diet is that you are not dieting all of the time. With only 2 days of restriction you can achieve a significant reduction in overall calories, whilst being flexible with food choices 5 days a week. Fasting days don't have to be consecutive, and you can change your 2 fasting days each week to fit in with your schedule and social engagements.

What are my calorie limits?

	Women	Men
Normal Day	2,000* Calories	2,500* Calories
Fasting Day	500 Calories	600 Calories

*Specific calorie requirements for a normal day vary from person to person, based on height, weight, age & activity level.

To calculate your calorie requirements & BMI, please visit:
www.carbsandcals.com/BMI

When prompted, please select 'maintain weight' as your weight goal to calculate your calorie requirements for a normal day.

What are the benefits of the 5:2 diet?

Many diets can be frustratingly difficult to follow, particularly if they restrict you to only a small number of foods, or cut out major food groups such as fat or starchy carbohydrate (e.g. bread, rice, pasta). Whether you have struggled with other diets that haven't worked, or are trying to lose weight for the first time, the 5:2 approach offers an alternative, easy-to-follow solution.

The 5:2 method is based on scientific research and there is a growing body of evidence to show that following the 5:2 diet offers many benefits. Reducing calories for only 2 days a week is easier for some people than traditional dieting for all 7 days. Fasting for 2 days a week can also help you understand portion control as, after 2 days of eating small amounts of food, people often realise that their usual portion sizes on non-fasting days are too large.

In addition, restricting your intake for only 2 days a week can lead to better insulin function, reduced cholesterol levels and fat loss rather than muscle loss. Intermittent fasting may also lead to greater reductions in insulin within the body, which has been linked to a lower risk of breast cancer. Additionally, fasting appears to help the body repair itself, which may slow the ageing process and prevent age-related mental deterioration.

What can I eat on the 2 fasting days?

Everyone is different; some people like to split their food intake on fasting days into 2 meals and 2 snacks, others like to have one larger meal a day – you know yourself best. Sometimes it takes a few fasting days to work out the most suitable plan for you. Foods that are good to include on fasting days are lean protein (e.g. meat, fish, eggs, tofu), low-fat and low-sugar dairy foods (e.g. skimmed milk, low-fat natural yogurt, cottage cheese), small amounts of healthy fats (e.g. almond butter, peanut butter, olive oil), vegetables and fruit.

You may be thinking *'What about carbs?'*. It is best to restrict carbohydrates, as they can make you more hungry. It's a good idea to eat plenty of protein as it has been scientifically proven to keep you feeling fuller for longer. Lots of vegetables can be included on your fast days as they are often very low in calories and high in nutrients. Salads are a great way to fill up your plate, while keeping within your calorie budget.

Calorie combinations on fasting days

If you are in a rush in the morning, with little time to prepare breakfast, it may be easier for you to skip breakfast and have:	**250 Cals** at lunch **250 Cals** for dinner
Busy at work through the day? Try missing lunch:	**250 Cals** for breakfast **250 Cals** for dinner
If you prefer the idea of three meals a day, have three smaller meals:	**150 Cals** for breakfast **150 Cals** at lunch **200 Cals** for dinner
Some people find that eating little and often works best to help keep hunger away through the day:	**100 Cals** for breakfast **50 Cals** for mid-morning snack **100 Cals** at lunch **50 Cals** for afternoon snack **200 Cals** for dinner

Top tips for fasting days

- Your fluid requirements are higher on a fast day, so drink more calorie-free fluids than normal. Aim for 3 litres on a fasting day. Water, herbal tea and sugar-free squash make great choices.

- Alcoholic drinks have little or no nutritional value and should be avoided on fasting days. Alcohol can make you feel more hungry and lead to a higher calorie intake than you had planned!

- Protein is very filling, so should be included where possible. Chicken, turkey, fish, pulses and beans are examples of high-protein, low-calorie options.

- Fill up on salad and vegetables as they are very low in calories.

What can I eat on the 5 non-fasting days?

The key to long term success when following the 5:2 diet is to maintain a balanced diet on your non-fast days. This ensures the hard work you put in is not wasted, and means you get a wide range of nutrients and vitamins. To achieve a balanced intake, include foods from all the main food groups:

Carbs	Choose wholegrain and low-GI varieties
Fruit & Veg	Make these a main part of each meal (5-a-day)
Dairy	Select low-fat options, e.g. skimmed milk & diet yogurt
Protein	Choose non-processed options such as eggs, meat, fish, nuts, beans & lentils
Fats	Use vegetable or olive oil in cooking. Limit fatty snacks such as chocolate, crisps, cakes & biscuits

One criticism of the 5:2 diet is that people do not always eat healthily on non-fast days. It is important to be aware of your recommended calorie limits on a normal day (see table on page 5). Use this book to help you understand calories in food and drinks, as overeating and having high-calorie items (e.g. take-away meals & alcohol) can easily take you over your recommended calories.

Top tips for non-fasting days

- Eat healthily 5 days a week, 3 meals a day. Balance is key.

- Snacks between meals should be healthy; yogurt and fruit are perfect as they are naturally low in calories and fat.

- Be mindful – is the food you are eating nourishing or junk food? Is the portion size right? Are you eating when you are full? Are you eating for reasons other than hunger?

- Try to cook foods yourself and cut down on processed foods.

- Allow yourself a treat, but avoid bingeing.

- Try to be active on your non-fasting days: walk to the shops, take the kids to the park or get out in the garden; it all counts. Consider how you can reduce the amount of sitting time each day, such as watching TV and time in front of a computer. Moving more will burn more calories.

Can anyone follow the 5:2 diet?

Measuring your Body Mass Index (BMI) is a good way to see if you need to lose weight. If you have a BMI higher than 25, following the 5:2 diet could help you to achieve a healthy weight.

To calculate your BMI, please visit:
www.carbsandcals.com/BMI

There are some people who should not follow the 5:2 diet; it is not recommended for those who are pregnant, breastfeeding or have an eating disorder. It is also unsuitable for children and adolescents. Approach your healthcare team for advice if you have low blood pressure, diabetes, kidney disease or depression.

Dietary restriction, of any type, can lead to nutritional deficiencies. Nutrients that you may lack on fasting days include calcium, iron and fibre. Take particular care to eat balanced meals and include sources of these nutrients on your non-fast days.

How to use this book

5:2 Diet Photos is a visual guide to help you achieve your 500 or 600 calorie target when following the 5:2 diet (it does not give detailed information on the 5:2 diet itself). For ease of use, the book is split into 3 sections: Recipes, Snacks and Individual Foods.

Recipes

The first part of the book contains 60 tasty recipes to use on your fast days, ranging from 105 to 385 calories. Each recipe is for 1 portion but can be scaled up for more people if required. They are quick to make, high in nutrients and low in calories. The  shows how many 5-a-day fruit & veg portions are in the recipe.

= 3 of your 5-a-day fruit & veg
[v] = vegetarian

Snacks

We have included a snack section, which includes 30 easy-to-prepare dishes, all under 100 calories.

Individual Foods

The remaining pages in the book contain over 500 individual food photos, showing the calories in a wide selection of popular foods. This information gives you the flexibility to create a meal plan that works for you, while still eating foods you enjoy. The visual method allows you to quickly select foods in appropriate portion sizes, to make up your 500 or 600 calorie allowance.

All of the above offers great support on fasting days, and can also be used on non-fasting days to maintain a healthy, balanced diet.

How do I use this book to create a meal plan?

1. Decide how you would like to split your calorie allowance for the day. For example, your 500 calories could be made up of:

> **200 Cals** for breakfast, **100 Cals** for a snack & **200 Cals** for dinner

2. Browse the book to decide what you want to eat for each meal. This may be a combination of **Recipes**, **Snacks** and foods from the **Individual Foods** section. Choose portions to stay within your calorie budget for each meal. Remember that all snacks and drinks must be taken into consideration.

3. Use the traffic light system, described opposite, to choose portions that are high in protein (to keep you feeling fuller) and low in fat. Try to get as many of your 5-a-day fruit & veg portions as you can, even on fasting days.

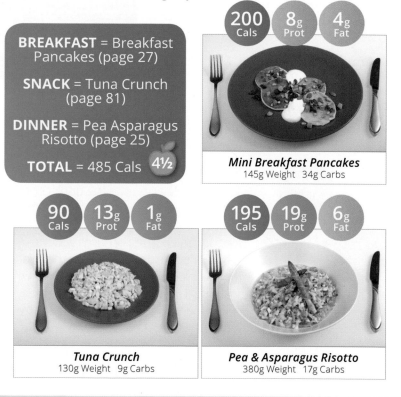

BREAKFAST = Breakfast Pancakes (page 27)

SNACK = Tuna Crunch (page 81)

DINNER = Pea Asparagus Risotto (page 25)

TOTAL = 485 Cals   4½

200 Cals 8g Prot 4g Fat

Mini Breakfast Pancakes
145g Weight   34g Carbs

90 Cals 13g Prot 1g Fat

Tuna Crunch
130g Weight   9g Carbs

195 Cals 19g Prot 6g Fat

Pea & Asparagus Risotto
380g Weight   17g Carbs

Traffic light system

The book uses a traffic light system for protein and fat. Foods high in protein will keep you fuller for longer, therefore you will see a green traffic light for foods with 10g or more of protein. Low-fat foods are generally healthier and more suitable for fasting days; foods with 2g of fat or less are displayed in green. The traffic light system makes it quick and easy to select healthy, filling foods.

	Green	Amber	Red
Protein	10g or above	5 - 9g	0 - 4g
Fat	0 - 2g	3 - 17g	18g or above

Judging portion sizes

To help with scale, each photo displays either a knife and fork or a dessert spoon. You might want to compare your dinnerware with that shown in the book. All food, recipes and snacks are displayed on plates or bowls of the following sizes:

26cm Dinner Plate

20cm Side Plate

22cm Large Bowl

14cm Cereal Bowl

The weight of each portion is always stated below the photo. You can use this to double-check your portion size by weighing your food.

Spicy aubergine stew [**v**]

105 Cals

400g WEIGHT   **20g** CARBS

Ingredients 3½

½ tsp **cumin seeds**

½ tsp **coriander seeds**

½ clove **garlic**, crushed

½ small **red onion** (40g), sliced

½ **red chilli**, sliced

130g **aubergine**, cubed

75g **carrot**, grated

½ tin **chopped tomatoes** (200g)

½ tsp **fresh mint**, chopped

½ tsp **fresh coriander**, chopped

5g Prot   **1g** Fat

Preparation

1. Toast the **cumin** and **coriander seeds** in a pan until they start to release their fragrant aroma

2. Grind the seeds to a powder in a pestle and mortar

3. Dry-fry the **garlic**, **onion** and **chilli** in a non-stick pan on a low heat, until the onion is soft and brown

4. Add the ground spices and **aubergine** to the pan with 150ml of water

5. Stir in the **carrot** and **tomatoes**, and bring to the boil

6. Reduce heat and simmer for 25 minutes

7. Mix through the **mint** and **coriander leaves**

8. To serve, garnish with a few additional mint leaves

Beef carpaccio

105
Cals

130g WEIGHT **3g** CARBS

Preparation

1. Mix the **rosemary** with the **black pepper**

2. Spoon half the mixture onto a chopping board

3. Place the fillet of **beef** on top of the mixture and firmly press down

4. Repeat steps 2 and 3, ensuring all sides of the beef are thoroughly coated

5. Pre-heat a non-stick frying pan until it is very hot

6. Sear each coated side of the beef for 1-2 minutes

7. Meanwhile, mix the **tomatoes**, **onions** and **watercress**

8. To serve, very thinly slice the beef and arrange with the watercress salad

Ingredients

1 tsp *fresh rosemary*, finely chopped

½ tsp *black peppercorns*, crushed

60g *beef fillet*, raw

50g *cherry tomatoes*, quartered

⅛ small *red onion* (10g), finely sliced

1 handful *watercress* (10g)

14g Prot   **4g** Fat

Butternut squash & mushroom soup [v]

110 Cals

415g WEIGHT **23g** CARBS

Ingredients

- ⅓ small **butternut squash** *(200g), peeled & cubed*
- 80g **chestnut mushrooms**, *halved*
- ¼ **red chilli**, *sliced*
- ½ tsp **fresh thyme**, *finely chopped*
- ½ tsp **fresh rosemary**, *finely chopped*
- 1 small **onion** *(70g), roughly chopped*
- 350ml **water**

Preparation

1. Add **all the ingredients** to a pan, season and bring to the boil

2. Simmer for 15-20 minutes, until the butternut squash is thoroughly cooked

3. Lightly blend, season to taste and serve

5g Prot   **1g** Fat

Tofu scramble [**v**]

130
Cals

260g WEIGHT   **11g** CARBS

Preparation

1. Add the **tomatoes**, **peppers** and **onion** to a frying pan and dry-fry for 3-5 minutes, until slightly tender

2. Add the **tofu** and heat through

3. Remove the pan from the heat and stir in the **parsley**

4. Serve on a plate and garnish with **rocket**

Ingredients

90g ***cherry tomatoes***, *quartered*

¼ ***green pepper*** *(25g), diced*

¼ ***red pepper*** *(25g), diced*

½ *small* ***red onion*** *(30g), diced*

150g ***silken tofu***, *crumbled*

1 tbsp ***flat-leaf parsley***, *roughly chopped*

1 *handful* ***rocket*** *(10g)*

13g Prot   **4g** Fat

140 Cals

Pathai prawn curry

355g WEIGHT   **12g** CARBS

Ingredients

*1 **red onion** (95g), sliced*

100g prawns, *raw*

1 tsp tamarind paste

*1 small handful **fresh coriander leaves***

For the masala paste

1 tsp coriander seeds

1½ tsp turmeric

½ tsp cumin seeds

*1 clove **garlic***

*1 dry **red chilli***

Preparation

1. Firstly, make the **masala paste** by adding all the **masala ingredients** to a food processor

2. Blend with 100ml water to make a thin paste

3. Add the paste along with the **onion**, **prawns**, **tamarind paste** and half the **fresh coriander** to a pan

4. Bring to the boil and simmer for approximately 8 minutes, until the prawns are cooked and the sauce has thickened

5. Serve garnished with the remaining coriander

20g Prot

1g Fat

Scallop, Parma ham & grapefruit salad

145 Cals

160g WEIGHT   8g CARBS

Preparation

1. Dry-fry the **scallops** for around 2-3 minutes on each side, until just cooked

2. Arrange the **rocket** on a plate with the **grapefruit** and **Parma ham**

3. Top with the scallops and serve

Ingredients

3 *large* **scallops** *(100g), raw*

20g *rocket*

70g *pink grapefruit* *segments*

1 *slice* **Parma ham** *(15g)*

22g Prot   3g Fat

Tom yum soup

160 Cals

335g WEIGHT   **9g** CARBS

Ingredients

350ml *vegetable stock*
(1 stock cube)

1 clove *garlic,*
finely chopped

1 inch *ginger,*
finely chopped

½ *lemongrass stalk,*
sliced

20g *carrot,* cut into
thin strips

40g *galangal,* sliced

140g *prawns,* raw

2 *kaffir lime leaves,*
roughly torn

Preparation

1. Add **all the ingredients** except the lime leaves to a pan and bring to the boil

2. Add the **lime leaves** and simmer for 3-5 minutes, until the prawns are cooked through

27g Prot   **3g** Fat

Tomato & chorizo soup with red pepper

175
Cals

370g WEIGHT   **13**g CARBS

Preparation

1. Add **all the ingredients** to a pan, season and bring to the boil

2. Simmer for 15-20 minutes

3. Lightly blend, season to taste and serve

Ingredients
2

*40g **chorizo**, cubed*

*1 small **tomato** (55g), quartered*

*½ **red onion** (45g), sliced*

*1 **red pepper** (100g), sliced*

*350ml **water***

9g Prot   **10**g Fat

Asian prawn salad

190 Cals

270g WEIGHT   **11g** CARBS

Ingredients

- ¼ **red chilli**, finely sliced
- ¼ **green chilli**, finely sliced
- ½ clove **garlic**, minced
- 125g **prawns**, raw
- 75g **bean sprouts**
- 80g **pak choi**, root removed
- 70g **carrot**, peeled into ribbons

32g Prot   **2g** Fat

Preparation

1. Add the **chilli**, **garlic** and **prawns** to a pan with 2 tbsp water

2. Cook until the prawns turn pink and are fully cooked (about 5 minutes)

3. Then add the **bean sprouts** to the pan and cook for 2 minutes

4. Meanwhile, layer the **pak choi** and **carrot** in a bowl

5. Serve the stir-fry on top of the layered salad

Cod with tomato & lemon thyme

190
Cals

345g WEIGHT   **8g** CARBS

Preparation

1. Add the **tomatoes**, **leek** and **thyme** to a pan with 100ml of water, and bring to the boil

2. Once boiling, slip the **cod** into the pan (making sure the fillet is covered by the sauce)

3. Gently simmer for 8-10 minutes, until the cod just begins to flake

4. Season to taste and serve

Ingredients

2

160g tinned **chopped tomatoes**

90g **leek**, sliced

½ tsp **lemon thyme**, finely chopped

180g **cod fillet** (sustainable), raw with skin removed

36g Prot

2g Fat

190 Cals

Steamed haddock & pak choi parcel

275g WEIGHT   **6g** CARBS

Ingredients 1½

95g *pak choi*

1 *lemongrass stalk*, *sliced lengthways*

1 *inch* **ginger**, *cut into matchsticks*

1 *red chilli, sliced*

195g *haddock fillet (sustainable), raw with skin removed*

2 tsp *lime juice*

39g Prot   **1g** Fat

Preparation

1. Pre-heat the oven to 200°C

2. Lay out enough tin foil to wrap the haddock and put a square of greaseproof paper on the inside

3. Place half the **pak choi** on the greaseproof paper and sprinkle with half the **lemongrass**, half the **ginger** and half the **chilli**

4. Place the **fish** on top and add the remaining lemongrass, chilli, ginger and pak choi

5. Seal the foil at the sides, leaving the top open

6. Pour the **lime juice** over the fish and seal the top of the foil to make a parcel

7. Place on an ovenproof tray and cook for 15 minutes, ensuring the fish is thoroughly cooked before serving

Mexican bean burger with spicy salsa [v]

190 Cals

340g WEIGHT   **34g** CARBS

Preparation

1. Pre-heat the oven to 200°C

2. Mix the **kidney beans**, **coriander** and **paprika** in a bowl

3. Mash with a potato masher then make into a patty

4. Cook on an oven tray for 10 minutes

5. To make the **salsa**, mix all of the **salsa ingredients** in a bowl and season

6. Place the **baby gem lettuce** on a plate with the sliced **tomato** and **red onion**

7. Once the burger is ready, place on the bed of salad and top with the salsa

8. Finish with sliced **beetroot**

Ingredients

4½

120g tinned **kidney beans**
1 tsp **fresh coriander**, chopped
½ tsp **smoked paprika**
35g **baby gem lettuce**
½ small **tomato** (30g), sliced
¼ small **red onion** (20g), sliced
60g cooked **beetroot**, sliced
For the salsa
¾ small **tomato** (45g), finely diced
¼ small **red onion** (20g), finely diced
½ **red chilli**, finely diced
2 tsp **lime juice**
1 tsp **fresh coriander**, chopped

12g Prot   **2g** Fat

Poached egg, smoked salmon & asparagus

195 Cals

215g WEIGHT   2g CARBS

Ingredients

80g asparagus

1 egg

2 tsp low-fat natural yogurt (10g)

1 tsp fresh dill, finely chopped

1 tsp lemon juice

50g wild Alaskan smoked salmon

Preparation

1. Cook the **asparagus** in boiling water for 2-3 minutes

2. Drain and immediately submerge in ice cold water

3. Poach an **egg**

4. To make the dressing, combine the **natural yogurt** with the **dill** and **lemon juice**

5. Serve the **smoked salmon**, asparagus and poached egg with the dressing on the side

24g Prot   10g Fat

Pea & asparagus risotto

195 Cals

380g WEIGHT   **17g** CARBS

Preparation

1. Boil the **peas** for 3 minutes until soft, then drain

2. Purée the peas in a food processor with salt, pepper and enough water to make a purée (around 50ml)

3. Remove the **asparagus** tips and reserve for later. Finely slice the stems, discarding any woody parts

4. Dry-fry the **onions** for 1 minute, before adding the **garlic** and 50ml of water. Add the sliced asparagus, along with the pea purée and heat for 1 minute

5. Add the **courgette** and **lemon thyme**, along with half the **Parma ham**, and cook for 2 minutes

6. Meanwhile, wrap the remaining Parma ham around the uncooked asparagus tips

7. Serve the risotto topped with the asparagus tips

Ingredients

110g *frozen peas*

65g *asparagus*

¼ *red onion* (25g), finely sliced

1 clove *garlic*, minced

120g *courgette*, very finely diced

1 tsp *lemon thyme*, finely chopped

2 slices *Parma ham* (25g)

19g Prot   **6g** Fat

200 Cals

Chicken stuffed with cherry tomatoes & basil

295g WEIGHT   **11g** CARBS

Ingredients

115g **chicken breast**, raw with skin removed

30g **cherry tomatoes**, quartered

1 handful **fresh basil**

80g **carrots**

80g **green beans**

1 handful **watercress** (10g)

Preparation

1. Pre-heat the oven to 200°C

2. Flatten the **chicken breast** using a rolling pin and lay the **cherry tomatoes** and **basil** in the middle

3. Roll the breast to encase the tomato filling, season with salt and pepper and place on a baking tray

4. Bake in the oven for 15-20 minutes, until the chicken is thoroughly cooked

5. Meanwhile, add the **carrots** to a pan of boiling water and simmer for 2 minutes

6. Add the **beans** and cook for a further 1-2 minutes, before draining

7. To serve, place the chicken on a bed of **watercress**, with the carrots and beans on the side

31g Prot   **4g** Fat

Mini breakfast pancakés [v]

200
Cals

145g WEIGHT **34g** CARBS

Preparation

1. Mix the **flour** and **icing sugar** together in a bowl

2. Gradually add the **milk**, while whisking to make a smooth batter

3. Heat a small non-stick frying pan on a high heat

4. Wipe the pan with a tiny amount of oil on a kitchen towel, or use an oil spray

5. Make 3-4 small pancakes

6. Serve the pancakes on a plate, spoon on the **yogurt** and sprinkle with the **dried fruit and seeds**

Ingredients

25g plain flour
2 tsp icing sugar
60ml skimmed milk
25g low-fat natural yogurt
15g mixed dried fruit and seeds

8g Prot

4g Fat

Corn chowder [**v**]

200 Cals

435g WEIGHT **39g** CARBS

Ingredients 2½

- **100g sweetcorn**, removed from cob
- **1 spring onion** (10g), sliced
- **1 small onion** (65g), diced
- **100g potato**, peeled & cubed
- **1 celery stick** (40g), finely sliced
- **½ tsp fresh thyme**, finely chopped
- **400ml vegetable stock** (½ stock cube)

7g Prot   **3g** Fat

Preparation

1. Add half the **corn** and **all of the other ingredients** to a pan with just enough of the **vegetable stock** to cover the vegetables, and bring to the boil

2. Meanwhile, add the remaining corn to a food processor with 2-3 tbsp stock and blitz

3. Add the blended corn to the pan containing the other veg (this adds a creamy texture to the dish)

4. Top up the pan with the remaining vegetable stock and cook until the potatoes are soft (15-20 minutes)

5. Lightly mash the potato to thicken the chowder

6. Season to taste and serve

Somerset stew [v]

200 Cals

460g WEIGHT   34g CARBS

Preparation

1. Add **all of the ingredients** to a pan

2. Bring to a boil and simmer on a medium heat for 20 minutes

3. Season to taste and serve

Ingredients 5

60g **black-eyed beans**

70g **butter beans**

1 large **celery stick** (50g), diced

1 small **onion** (65g), finely diced

80g **leek**, sliced

250ml **vegetable stock** (⅓ stock cube)

½ tsp **fresh thyme**, finely chopped

100g tinned **chopped tomatoes**

2 tsp **tomato purée** (10g)

14g Prot   **2**g Fat

Beetroot & goat's cheese medley [v]

215 **Cals**

335g WEIGHT   **18g** CARBS

Ingredients

225g **beetroot**, cubed
(can be raw or cooked;
if using raw beetroot,
peel first)

40g **goat's cheese**,
crumbled

25g **pea shoots**

Preparation

1. Mix the **beetroot** and **goat's cheese** together and season with salt and pepper

2. Place the mixture on a bed of **pea shoots**

13g Prot   **11g** Fat

Tuna Niçoise

220 Cals

260g WEIGHT **3g** CARBS

Preparation

1. Boil the **egg** in simmering water for 8 minutes

2. Remove the egg from the water, leave to cool, then de-shell and slice

3. To make the dressing, combine the **natural yogurt** with the **dill** and **lemon juice**

4. To prepare the salad, lay a bed of **rocket** on a plate with the **tuna**, **cherry tomatoes**, **capers** and egg, and top with the yogurt dressing

Ingredients

1 *egg*

2 tsp *low-fat natural yogurt (10g)*

1 tsp *fresh dill, finely chopped*

1 tsp *lemon juice*

35g *rocket*

100g *tuna (tinned in water), drained*

40g *cherry tomatoes, halved*

1 tbsp *capers*

34g Prot **8g** Fat

Lemon-chilli chicken with butternut squash

225
Cals

280g WEIGHT   **26g** CARBS

Ingredients

- ½ small **butternut squash** (280g), cubed
- ½ **red chilli**, sliced
- ¼ **lemon** (zest & juice)
- 85g **chicken breast**, raw, diced
- ½ tsp **fresh thyme**, finely chopped
- ½ tsp **oregano**, fresh or dried
- 1 tsp **Greek yogurt** (0% fat)
- 1 handful **baby spinach** (15g)

27g Prot   **2g** Fat

Preparation

1. Place the **squash** on a baking tray, season and put in the oven for 30-40 minutes

2. Mix the **chilli** with the **lemon zest and juice**, **chicken**, **thyme** and **oregano**, and leave to marinate for at least 30 minutes

3. Combine the chicken with the butternut squash and return to the oven for 15-20 minutes, until the chicken is thoroughly cooked

4. Stir through the **Greek yogurt** and serve on a bed of **baby spinach**

Foil-wrapped sea bass with fennel

225
Cals

325g WEIGHT   **8g** CARBS

Preparation

1. Pre-heat the oven to 200°C

2. Take some baking parchment and a large piece of foil, laying the paper on top of the foil

3. Layer the **fennel**, **peppers**, **onion** and **olives** on the paper and place the **sea bass** on top (skin side up)

4. Season with salt and pepper

5. Add the **lemon slices** to the sea bass skin and sprinkle with **dill**

6. Seal in the foil and bake for 15-20 minutes until thoroughly cooked

Ingredients

45g **fennel**, finely sliced

¼ **red pepper** (25g), finely sliced

¼ **green pepper** (25g), finely sliced

½ small **red onion** (35g), finely sliced

70g **pitted green olives** (in brine), halved

125g **sea bass fillet**, raw

4 thin slices of **lemon**

1 tsp **fresh dill**, chopped

27g
Prot

10g
Fat

Pork & mushroom Stroganoff

230 Cals

230g WEIGHT **12g** CARBS

Ingredients

- 1 clove **garlic**, minced
- ½ **red onion** (50g), sliced
- 70g **chestnut mushrooms**, sliced
- 70g **oyster mushrooms**, sliced
- 50g **shiitake mushrooms**, sliced
- 75g **pork tenderloin**, raw, in small cubes
- 1 tsp **paprika**
- 1 tsp **chives**, chopped
- 1 tsp **flat-leaf parsley**, chopped
- 20g **soured cream**

24g Prot   **10g** Fat

Preparation

1. Add the **garlic** to a pan with the **onion**, **mushrooms** and 50ml of water

2. Cover and bring to the boil

3. Reduce the heat and simmer for 5-7 minutes, until everything has cooked down

4. Mix through the **pork**, **paprika**, half the **chives**, half the **parsley**, and season

5. Cook for 5 minutes more, until the pork is tender

6. Just before serving, stir in the **soured cream** and garnish with the remaining parsley and chives

Prawn pad Thai

235 Cals

255g WEIGHT **23g** CARBS

Preparation

1. Add the **carrot**, **chilli**, **ginger**, **garlic** and **prawns** to a hot wok with half the **spring onions** and a splash of water

2. Cook for 2 minutes

3. Add the **bean sprouts** and **fish sauce** to the wok and fry for a further 2 minutes

4. Crush the **peanuts** and add them to the wok with another splash of water

5. Season with salt and pepper

6. Mix through the **rice noodles**, and heat for a further 1-2 minutes

7. Add the remaining spring onions, **lime juice** and **coriander**, stir and serve

Ingredients 1½

30g *carrot*, cut into batons
½ *red chilli*, finely chopped
½ inch *ginger*, finely chopped
½ clove *garlic*, finely chopped
80g *prawns*, raw
3 *spring onions* (30g), sliced
40g *bean sprouts*
1 tsp *fish sauce*
10g *unsalted peanuts*
60g straight-to-wok *rice noodles*
2 tsp *lime juice*
½ tsp *fresh coriander*, chopped

20g Prot   **7g** Fat

235 Cals

Pineapple prawn stir-fry

410g WEIGHT   19g CARBS

Ingredients 4

1 pack **stir-fry vegetables** (285g), ready-prepared

100g **prawns**, cooked

1 tsp **Chinese 5-spice**

60g fresh **pineapple** chunks

1 tbsp **soy sauce**

Preparation

1. Dry-fry the **stir-fry vegetables** in a hot, non-stick pan for 2-3 minutes

2. Add the **prawns, Chinese 5-spice, pineapple** and **soy sauce**

3. Cook for a further 1-2 minutes and serve

31g Prot   3g Fat

Turkey & veg ragù

235
Cals

485g WEIGHT **17g** CARBS

Preparation

1. Dry-fry the **onions** and **garlic** in a non-stick pan for 1-2 minutes, stirring continuously to prevent sticking and burning

2. Add the **pepper, beans** and **courgette** to the pan, along with 100ml water, and bring to the boil

3. Mix in the **turkey** and **tomatoes**, and bring back to the boil

4. Season with salt and pepper, and simmer on a medium heat for 10-15 minutes until the sauce has thickened

5. Just before serving, stir through the **herbs** and finish with **parmesan** (optional)

Ingredients 4

½ small **red onion** (30g), diced

1 clove **garlic**, minced

1 small **red pepper** (80g), diced

40g **green beans**, halved

80g **courgette**, diced

120g **turkey breast**, raw, diced

200g tinned **chopped tomatoes**

½ tsp **oregano**, fresh or dried

1 tsp **basil**, fresh or dried

1 tsp **parmesan**, grated

36g Prot

3g Fat

Chicken & prawn paella

235 **Cals**

605g WEIGHT **14g** CARBS

Ingredients

60g **prawns**, *raw*

80g **chicken breast**, *raw, diced*

1 tsp **paprika**

120g **courgette**, *very finely diced*

½ **red pepper** (50g), *diced*

¼ **yellow pepper** (25g), *diced*

½ **lemon** *(zest & juice)*

80g **cherry tomatoes**, *halved*

½ **chicken stock cube**

2 tsp **tomato purée** (10g)

36g Prot **4g** Fat

Preparation

1. Place the **prawns** and **chicken** into a pan, along with the **paprika** and 50ml water

2. Cook for 2 minutes on a medium-high heat

3. Add the **remaining ingredients** with a further 150ml water and bring to the boil

4. Allow to simmer for 10-12 minutes before serving

Egg & spinach on rye [v]

240 Cals

190g WEIGHT 28g CARBS

Preparation

1. Place the **spinach**, with 1 tbsp water, into a pan on a medium heat and wilt for 1-2 minutes

2. Meanwhile, toast the **rye bread** and poach the **egg**

3. To serve, place the wilted spinach onto the toast and top with the egg

4. Season with salt and pepper to taste

Ingredients

60g **spinach**

2 thin slices **rye bread** (60g)

1 **egg**

14g Prot   **8g** Fat

Cheesy breakfast mushroom stack [**v**]

240 Cals

195g WEIGHT   3g CARBS

Ingredients

- 2 **portobello mushrooms** *(140g)*
- ½ **red Romano pepper** *(35g), sliced*
- 1 clove **garlic**, *finely diced*
- 50g **smoked cheddar cheese**, *sliced*
- 1 *handful* **watercress** *(10g)*

Preparation

1. Pre-heat the oven to 180°C

2. Lay one **mushroom** topside down on a baking tray

3. Place half the **peppers** on the mushroom, sprinkle with half the **garlic** and season with salt and pepper

4. Add the sliced **cheese**, then the other half of the peppers and the rest of the garlic to make a stack

5. Place the other mushroom on top and apply a small amount of pressure

6. Cook for 12-15 minutes in the oven, turning once half way through cooking

7. Serve garnished with **watercress**

16g Prot   **18**g Fat

Seared beef & mushroom salad

240 Cals

260g WEIGHT   **13g** CARBS

Preparation

1. Add **all the ingredients** except the rocket to a sauté pan, along with 100ml water

2. Cover the pan and simmer for around 6-8 minutes

3. Using a slotted spoon, remove the ingredients from the pan, leaving the liquid

4. Reduce the liquid in the same pan for about a minute to make a thin gravy, then remove from the heat

5. Serve the beef and vegetables on a bed of **rocket**, drizzled with the tasty sauce

Ingredients 2

125g *beef fillet*, raw, trimmed of fat and sliced

60g *chestnut mushrooms*, quartered

1 clove ***garlic*,** finely sliced

60g tinned ***kidney beans***

½ tsp *fresh rosemary*, finely chopped

35g *rocket*

34g Prot   **6g** Fat

245 **Cals**

Turkey meatballs in a Mediterranean sauce

420g WEIGHT **15g** CARBS

Ingredients 3½

150g **turkey mince**, *raw*

1 tsp **fresh thyme**, *chopped*

½ small **onion** *(20g), finely diced*

1 clove **garlic**, *minced*

½ large **yellow pepper** *(60g), diced*

½ large **red pepper** *(60g), diced*

80g **courgette**, *diced*

40g **aubergine**, *diced*

1 handful **fresh basil**

50g **passata**

41g Prot   **2g** Fat

Preparation

1. Add the **turkey**, **thyme** and half the **onions** to a bowl with salt and pepper, and thoroughly mix

2. Roll the mixture into 4-6 meatballs

3. Dry-fry the remaining onions and **garlic** in a pan on a high heat for 3 minutes

4. Add the **remaining vegetables** and **basil**, cover with **passata** and cook for 7-10 minutes on a medium heat

5. Gently place the meatballs on top of the sauce (but don't stir)

6. Cover and cook for a further 8 minutes until the meatballs are thoroughly cooked

Pork tenderloin with black bean sauce

245 Cals

225g WEIGHT   **7g** CARBS

Preparation

1. Add the **sesame oil** to a pan along with the **ginger**, **garlic**, **chilli**, **black beans** and **rice wine vinegar**

2. Heat for 2-3 minutes on a medium heat

3. Pour in 150ml water and the sliced **pork**

4. Bring to the boil and then simmer for 10 minutes, until the pork is tender

5. Meanwhile, boil the **broccoli** for 3-5 minutes

6. Season to taste and serve

Ingredients

½ tsp **sesame oil**

½ inch **ginger**, minced

1 clove **garlic**, minced

½ **red chilli**, finely chopped

90g tinned **black beans**

1 tsp **rice wine vinegar**

100g **pork tenderloin**, raw, sliced

80g **broccoli**, cut into florets

29g Prot   **10g** Fat

245 Cals

Spinach bacon pasta & slow-roasted tomatoes

200g WEIGHT **37g** CARBS

Ingredients 2

100g *cherry tomatoes*, halved

½ tsp *fresh thyme*, finely chopped

½ tsp *fresh rosemary*, finely chopped

1 clove *garlic*, finely diced

50g *wholemeal spaghetti*

40g *smoked back bacon*, raw, fat removed

25g *baby spinach*

16g Prot   **5g** Fat

Preparation

1. Pre-heat the oven to 120°C

2. Mix the **tomatoes** with the **thyme**, **rosemary** and **garlic**, then season with salt and pepper

3. Roast on a baking tray in the oven for 90 minutes

4. Once the tomatoes are cooked, place the **spaghetti** in a large pan of boiling water and cook for 8-10 minutes until tender

5. Meanwhile, grill the **bacon** and slice into lardons

6. Drain the spaghetti and mix together with the **spinach**, tomatoes and bacon

7. Season to taste and serve

Linguine with turkey & chestnut mushrooms

245 Cals

200g WEIGHT   **27**g CARBS

Preparation

1. Cook the **linguine** or **spaghetti** according to packet instructions and drain

2. Add the **mushrooms** and **turkey** to a separate pan with 1tbsp water and the **oregano**

3. Cook on a medium-high heat for 5-7 minutes, until the turkey is cooked

4. Combine the cooked pasta with the turkey mixture

5. Sprinkle on the **parmesan**, stir through and serve

Ingredients

40g *linguine* or *wholemeal spaghetti*

80g *chestnut mushrooms, sliced*

60g *turkey breast, raw, sliced*

1 tsp *oregano, dried or fresh*

10g *parmesan, grated*

25g Prot   **5**g Fat

255
Cals

3 Bean salad [**v**]

315g WEIGHT   **42g** CARBS

Ingredients 4

- 60g tinned **borlotti beans**
- 70g tinned **red kidney beans**
- 70g tinned **black-eyed beans**
- 1 handful **flat-leaf parsley**, chopped
- ½ small **red onion** (20g), finely sliced
- 1 clove **garlic**, minced
- ½ **lemon** (zest & juice)
- 1 tbsp **white wine vinegar**
- 70g **mixed salad leaves**

Preparation

1. Add **all the beans** to a large bowl along with the **parsley**, **red onion** and **garlic**

2. Add in the **lemon zest and juice**, along with the **white wine vinegar**

3. Season with salt and pepper and mix well

4. Leave to stand for at least 5 minutes, to allow the flavours to infuse

5. Mix with the **salad leaves** and serve

19g Prot   **2g** Fat

Baked egg ratatouille [**v**]

255 Cals

410g WEIGHT **30g** CARBS

Preparation

1. Pre-heat the oven to 200°C

2. Place **all the ingredients** except the egg into a roasting tin and season with salt and pepper

3. Make an indentation in the vegetable mix and crack an **egg** into the dimple

4. Bake for 25-30 minutes

Ingredients

1 small **red pepper** (70g), diced

1 small **yellow pepper** (70g), diced

1 small **red onion** (75g), sliced

180g **plum tomatoes**, quartered

150g **passata**

1 clove **garlic**, sliced

1 tsp **fresh thyme**, chopped

1 **egg**

14g Prot **9g** Fat

255 Cals

Slow-roasted tomato & chorizo salad

220g WEIGHT **13g** CARBS

Ingredients

100g *cherry tomatoes*, halved

½ tsp *fresh rosemary*, finely chopped

1 clove *garlic*, finely diced

1 tsp *fresh thyme*, finely chopped

100g *chestnut mushrooms*, quartered

45g *chorizo*, sliced

50ml *Marsala wine*

20g *baby spinach*

15g *rocket*

12g Prot **12g** Fat

Preparation

1. Pre-heat the oven to 120°C

2. Mix the **tomatoes** with the **rosemary**, **garlic** and half the **thyme**, then season with salt and pepper

3. Place onto a baking tray and roast in the oven for 90 minutes

4. Meanwhile, dry-fry the **mushrooms** in a pan with the **chorizo**, remaining thyme and freshly ground black pepper, until the mushrooms are tender

5. Add the **Marsala wine**, reduce down (this will only take a few seconds), then remove the pan from the heat

6. Mix the tomatoes with the mushrooms and chorizo. Serve on a bed of **spinach** and **rocket**

Chickpea lentil curry [v]

260 Cals

350g WEIGHT **43g** CARBS

Preparation

1. Soak the **lentils** in water for at least 10 minutes

2. Rub the lentils between your fingers to remove the outer husk, then drain and rinse with water

3. Add **all the ingredients** except the parsley to a pan

4. Season, then simmer on a medium heat for 25 minutes until the lentils are cooked

5. Add the **parsley** to the curry, stir through and serve

Ingredients

3

*40g dry **yellow lentils***

*60g tinned **chickpeas***

*½ **red onion** (55g), sliced*

*½ tin **plum tomatoes** (200g)*

*1 medium **fresh tomato** (90g), quartered*

*2 tsp **lime juice***

*½ **red chilli**, chopped*

*½ tsp **chilli powder***

*1 tsp **flat-leaf parsley**, roughly chopped*

18g Prot   **3g** Fat

Butter bean, tomato & fennel salad [v]

260 Cals

405g WEIGHT   30g CARBS

Ingredients 5

70g *fennel*, finely sliced

80g *pitted green olives (in brine)*, quartered

200g tinned *butter beans*

80g *cherry tomatoes*, quartered

80g *watercress*

Preparation

1. Place the **fennel**, **olives** and **butter beans** into a bowl and mix thoroughly

2. Sprinkle the **tomatoes** and **watercress** on top, season to taste and serve

16g Prot

9g Fat

Poached salmon with chilli-roasted squash

265
Cals

205g WEIGHT   **12g** CARBS

Preparation

1. Pre-heat the oven to 200°C

2. Mix the **squash**, **chilli**, **mushrooms** and **sage**

3. Season and place on a baking tray

4. Cook for 20-30 minutes, until the squash is cooked

5. Meanwhile, bring a pan of water to the boil and add the **lemon** and **dill**

6. Add the **salmon** and simmer gently for 5-8 minutes until cooked

7. Serve the salmon on top of the butternut squash and mushrooms, garnished with **rocket**

Ingredients

¼ **butternut squash** (140g), peeled & diced

1 **green chilli**, finely diced

70g **chestnut mushrooms**, quartered

½ tsp **dried sage**

½ **lemon**

2 sprigs of **fresh dill**

115g **salmon fillet**, raw

1 small handful **rocket** (5g)

26g
Prot

13g
Fat

265
Cals

Salmon fishcake with spinach & fennel salad

270g WEIGHT   **26g** CARBS

Ingredients 1

80g salmon fillet, raw with skin removed

140g new potatoes, diced

¼ red onion (25g), sliced

1 tsp fresh dill, chopped

1 tsp lemon juice

½ red chilli, sliced

45g fennel, sliced

25g baby spinach

Preparation

1. Pre-heat the oven to 200°C

2. Bake the **salmon** for 10 minutes

3. Meanwhile, boil the **potatoes** until soft

4. Add the **onion**, **dill**, **lemon juice**, **chilli**, cooked salmon and new potatoes to a large bowl

5. Mash with a potato masher until thoroughly mixed and form into a good sized patty

6. Cook in the oven for 10 minutes

7. Arrange the **fennel** on a plate with the **spinach**, and top with the fishcake

20g Prot

10g Fat

Chunky cottage pie

275 **Cals**

440g WEIGHT   **29g** CARBS

Preparation

1. Add the **onion**, **garlic**, **beef**, **carrot**, **peas** and **herbs** to the pan and dry-fry for 5 minutes

2. Pour in the **beef stock** and leave to simmer for around 15 minutes, until thickened

3. Meanwhile, boil a separate pan of water. Add the **potatoes** and boil for around 10-15 minutes, until soft

4. Crush down the new potatoes lightly with a fork

5. Blanch the **savoy cabbage** for 3-5 minutes, until tender

6. Add the beef mix to a plate, top with the potato and serve with the cabbage on the side

Ingredients   2

½ *small **onion** (40g), sliced*

1 *clove **garlic**, minced*

100g ***sirloin steak**, raw, diced*

50g ***carrots**, sliced*

25g ***peas***

1 tsp ***fresh rosemary**, chopped*

1 tsp ***fresh thyme**, chopped*

100ml ***beef stock** (⅓ stock cube)*

100g ***new potatoes**, diced*

55g ***savoy cabbage**, sliced*

29g Prot

6g Fat

Chicken with mango & lime salsa

280 Cals

340g WEIGHT   **19g** CARBS

Ingredients

150g **chicken breast**, raw, skinless

80g **mango**, finely diced

1 **red chilli**, finely sliced

½ **lime** (zest & juice)

1 small handful **flat-leaf parsley**, finely chopped

70g **baby spinach**

Preparation

1. Pre-heat the oven to 180°C

2. Season the **chicken** with salt and pepper

3. Place on a baking tray and into the oven for 12-15 minutes, or until thoroughly cooked

4. Meanwhile, mix the **mango**, **chilli**, **lime** and **parsley** in a bowl to make the salsa

5. To serve, arrange the **spinach** in a large bowl, add the cooked chicken and dress with the mango salsa

41g Prot   **5g** Fat

Stuffed aubergine with bulgur wheat & feta [v]

280 Cals

325g WEIGHT **36g** CARBS

Preparation

1. Pre-heat the oven to 200°C

2. Cook the **bulgur wheat** according to packet instructions and drain

3. Bake the **aubergine** for 10 minutes

4. Mix the bulgur wheat with the **tomatoes, feta, herbs** and **olives**

5. Add ¾ of the mixture to the aubergine and place it back into the oven for around 15-20 minutes

6. Serve with the remaining bulgur wheat mixture on the side

Ingredients 2

40g **bulgur wheat,** uncooked

½ **aubergine** (80g)

65g **cherry tomatoes,** quartered

30g **feta cheese,** cubed

½ tsp **fresh oregano,** finely chopped

½ tsp **fresh rosemary,** finely chopped

½ tsp **fresh basil,** finely chopped

30g **pitted green olives** (in brine), chopped

12g Prot   **11g** Fat

285 Cals

Tuna steak with stir-fried vegetables

430g WEIGHT   **14g** CARBS

Ingredients 4

- **110g** *pak choi*, root removed, halved lengthways
- ½ *small **red onion** (30g), finely sliced*
- **50g** *carrot*, sliced lengthways
- **70g** *mangetout*
- **60g** *fennel*, finely sliced
- ½ *inch **ginger**, minced*
- ½ *clove **garlic**, minced*
- ¼ *lime (zest & juice)*
- **1** *red chilli*, finely sliced
- **150g** *tuna steak*, raw

41g Prot   **8g** Fat

Preparation

1. Cut the root off the **pak choi**, separate the leaves and cut down the middle

2. Pre-heat a deep pan or wok until very hot

3. Add the pak choi, **onion**, **carrot**, **mangetout** and **fennel** with a small amount of water and cook on a high heat for 1 minute

4. Add the **ginger**, **garlic**, **lime zest and juice**, and half the **red chilli**. Cook on a high heat for a further 5 minutes

5. Meanwhile, heat a non-stick pan over a medium-high heat and sear the **tuna steak** for 3 minutes on each side, or until it is cooked to your liking

6. Serve the tuna on the stir-fried vegetables and top with slices of chilli

Beef pasanda

290 Cals

230g WEIGHT   **13g** CARBS

Preparation

1. Mix **all the dry spices** with the **Greek yogurt**

2. Stir in the **beef** and put into the fridge

3. Allow to marinate for at least 30 minutes

4. Heat the **oil** in a pan and slowly fry the **onion**, **garlic** and **ginger**, until the onion is soft

5. Add the **tomatoes** and cook for a further 1-2 minutes

6. Stir through the beef and yogurt mixture, and simmer gently for 10-15 minutes

7. Serve garnished with **coriander**

Ingredients

½ *tsp* **cumin seeds**
½ *tsp* **ground coriander**
½ *tsp* **chilli powder**
¼ *tsp* **turmeric**
45g **Greek yogurt** *(0% fat)*
120g **beef fillet**, *raw, thinly sliced*
1 *tsp* **olive oil**
½ **red onion** *(55g), sliced*
1 *clove* **garlic**, *minced*
1 *inch* **ginger**, *minced*
70g **plum tomatoes**, *chopped*
1 *handful* **fresh coriander**

33g Prot   **12g** Fat

290 Cals

Beef & vegetable stew

420g WEIGHT   **29g** CARBS

Ingredients

100g **sirloin steak**, raw, diced

½ small **red onion** (40g), sliced

1 clove **garlic**, minced

60g **peas**

35g **carrots**, sliced

40g **green beans**, halved

60g **new potatoes**, diced

45g tinned **chopped tomatoes**

250ml **beef stock** (½ stock cube)

1 tsp **fresh rosemary**, chopped

Preparation

1. Add **all the ingredients** to a pan, seasoning with salt and pepper

2. Bring to the boil, cover and simmer gently for 15 minutes

3. Remove the lid and continue simmering for a further 10-15 minutes, to allow the stock to reduce

31g Prot

6g Fat

Breakfast bean burrito [v]

290 Cals

250g WEIGHT 34g CARBS

Preparation

1. Add **all the ingredients**, except the egg and the wrap, to a hot pan with a tablespoon of water

2. Cook for around 5 minutes, until the vegetables have sweated down

3. Add the **egg** and keep stirring so the egg scrambles

4. Place the egg and bean mixture onto the **wrap**, fold in one end and roll into a burrito

5. Serve any extra filling on the side

Ingredients

30g **cherry tomatoes**, quartered

⅓ **yellow pepper** (30g), diced

⅓ **green pepper** (30g), diced

½ small **red onion** (30g), diced

65g tinned **kidney beans**

1 **egg**

1 mini **wholemeal tortilla wrap** (32g)

16g Prot   10g Fat

295
Cals

Spiced turkey breast with parsnip chips

265g WEIGHT   **18g** CARBS

Ingredients

½ tsp **ground cumin**

½ tsp **cinnamon**

160g **turkey breast**, raw

80g **parsnips**,
cut into thin batons

½ tsp **olive oil**

1 clove **garlic**, minced

80g **broccoli**

1 tsp **cranberry sauce**

Preparation

1. Pre-heat the oven to 180°C

2. Mix the **cumin** and **cinnamon** together with salt and pepper. Rub the spices into the **turkey breast** on a non-stick baking tray. Roast in the oven for 30 minutes, turning half way through

3. Meanwhile, place the **parsnips** into a bowl and mix with the **olive oil** and **garlic**

4. Lay the parsnip chips onto a baking tray and cook for 20 minutes, shaking half way through

5. While the turkey and parsnips are cooking, bring a saucepan of water to the boil and cook the **broccoli** in simmering water for 4-5 minutes

6. Serve the turkey, parsnips and broccoli with the **cranberry sauce** on the side

45g Prot   **5g** Fat

Spicy fish with lentils

295 **Cals**

300g WEIGHT **27g** CARBS

Preparation

1. Pre-heat the oven to 180°C

2. Place a section of baking parchment onto a large piece of foil and position the **cod** on top

3. Sprinkle the cod with **cayenne pepper**. Lay the slice of **lemon** on top and seal the cod into a foil parcel. Bake for 10-12 minutes, until thoroughly cooked

4. Meanwhile, fry the **onion** and **celery** in the **olive oil** on a low heat for around 7 minutes

5. Cook the **puy lentils** according to packet instructions

6. Mix the lentils with the onion and celery

7. To serve, place the fish on the bed of lentils and sprinkle with **parsley**

Ingredients

140g cod loin (sustainable), raw with skin removed

1 tsp cayenne pepper

1 slice **lemon**

1 small **red onion** (60g), finely diced

1 **celery stick** (40g), finely diced

½ tsp **olive oil**

100g puy lentils, uncooked

1 tsp **flat-leaf parsley**, chopped

38g Prot   **5g** Fat

300 Cals

Chinese-style prawn omelette

285g WEIGHT   **7g** CARBS

Ingredients

½ tsp *olive oil*

½ *red pepper* (50g), sliced

½ small *red chilli*, thinly sliced

1 clove *garlic*, sliced

80g *bean sprouts*

2 *eggs*

1 tsp *light soy sauce*

1 tsp *rice wine vinegar*

50g *prawns*, cooked

Preparation

1. Heat the **oil** in a pan, on a medium heat.

2. Fry the **pepper**, **chilli** and **garlic** for a few minutes

3. Add the **bean sprouts** and cook for 2 more minutes

4. Take the vegetables out of the pan and set aside

5. Whisk together the **eggs**, **soy sauce** and **vinegar**

6. Return the pan to the heat and pour in the egg mixture. As the egg begins to set, lay the vegetables and **prawns** on one half and fold the omelette over

7. Let it cook for a further minute and serve

30g Prot

17g Fat

Pecan breakfast pot [**v**]

300 Cals

395g WEIGHT **39g** CARBS

Preparation

1. Prepare **all the fruit** and place into a large bowl

2. Pour over the **yogurt**, top with **pomegranate** and **pecan nuts**, and serve

Ingredients

60g *pineapple*, cubed

80g *strawberries*, quartered

60g *raspberries*

50g *blueberries*

100g *low-fat natural yogurt*

70g *pomegranate seeds*

15g *pecans*

10g Prot **13**g Fat

305 Cals

Couscous, feta & pomegranate salad [v]

265g WEIGHT   **43g** CARBS

Ingredients

- **50g giant wholewheat couscous**, uncooked
- **1 tbsp fresh mint**, chopped
- **40g cherry tomatoes**, halved
- **40g pomegranate seeds**
- **40g feta cheese**, cubed
- **1 tsp harissa paste**

Preparation

1. Cook the **couscous** according to packet instructions and leave to cool

2. Mix the **mint**, **cherry tomatoes**, **pomegranate** and **feta** in a separate bowl

3. Once the couscous has cooled, stir through the **harissa paste**

4. Combine everything together and serve

13g Prot   **10g** Fat

Egg whites & homemade baked beans [v]

310 Cals

360g WEIGHT **52g** CARBS

Preparation

1. Add **all the ingredients**, except the egg whites, bread and parsley, to a pan with 50ml water

2. Cover and cook on a medium heat for 20-30 minutes, stirring occasionally

3. Meanwhile, place a non-stick pan on a high heat and add the **egg whites**

4. Cook until the egg turns white and is still moist

5. Scramble with a spatula

6. Place the egg whites on a slice of **sourdough bread** with the beans on the side

7. Garnish with **parsley** and serve

Ingredients 3½

75g tinned **cannellini beans**

65g tinned **kidney beans**

120g tinned **plum tomatoes**

½ small **red onion** (35g), diced

1 tbsp **white wine vinegar**

1½ tsp **Demerara sugar**

2 **egg whites**

1 small slice **sourdough bread** (30g)

½ tsp **flat-leaf parsley**, chopped

21g Prot

2g Fat

Smoked salmon roulade

315 Cals

160g WEIGHT   **31g** CARBS

Ingredients

½ tsp **fresh dill**, *finely chopped*

20g **soured cream**

1 tsp **lemon juice**

1 small **seeded tortilla** *(62g)*

1 handful **rocket** *(10g)*

60g **smoked salmon**

Preparation

1. Mix the **dill**, **soured cream** and **lemon juice** in a bowl, and season with salt and pepper

2. Spread the mixture on the **tortilla** and add the **rocket** and **smoked salmon**

3. Roll the tortilla and slice down the middle

4. Serve on a bed of rocket

22g Prot

11g Fat

Cajun-spiced chicken quinoa salad

320 Cals

265g WEIGHT **38g** CARBS

Preparation

1. Cut the **chicken** into small, bite-sized pieces

2. Sprinkle with the **Cajun seasoning**

3. Dry-fry for 8-10 minutes until cooked

4. Cook the **quinoa** according to packet instructions, drain and set aside

5. Mix the **beetroot** into the quinoa

6. For the dressing, mix the **yogurt**, **lemon juice**, and half the **coriander**, seasoning with salt and pepper

7. Serve the chicken on the quinoa, topped with the yogurt dressing and the remaining coriander

Ingredients ½

100g **chicken breast**, raw with skin removed

1 tsp **Cajun seasoning**

50g **red** or **white quinoa**, uncooked

35g cooked **beetroot**, cubed

20g **low-fat natural yogurt**

1 tbsp **fresh coriander**, chopped

1 tsp **lemon juice**

33g Prot **4g** Fat

325 Cals

Spanish frittata [**v**]

365g WEIGHT **29g** CARBS

Ingredients

135g **potato**, peeled & sliced

1 small **onion** (65g), sliced

½ tsp **flat-leaf parsley**, chopped

2 **eggs**

40g **cherry tomatoes**, halved

1 handful **rocket** (10g)

20g Prot

15g Fat

Preparation

1. Pre-heat the oven to 200°C

2. Place the **potatoes** and **onion** into a pan and cover with water

3. Gently boil until the potato is tender (around 8-10 minutes), then drain off the water

4. Add the cooked potato, onion and **parsley** to a non-stick ovenproof dish, or one lined with greaseproof paper

5. Whisk the **eggs**, season with salt and pepper, and pour over the potato and onions

6. Cook in the oven for around 15-20 minutes, until the egg has risen and set

7. Serve garnished with **cherry tomatoes** and **rocket**

Mackerel salad with beetroot & walnuts

345 Cals

245g WEIGHT **10g** CARBS

Preparation

1. Lay the **spinach** on a plate and place the **mackerel** on top

2. Arrange the **beetroot**, **celery** and **walnuts**

3. Serve with the **creamed horseradish** on the side

Ingredients

50g *baby spinach*

70g *peppered smoked mackerel fillet*

80g *cooked beetroot, sliced*

1 *small celery stick (30g), sliced*

10g *walnuts, crushed*

1 tsp *creamed horseradish*

19g Prot **25g** Fat

Chickpea patty with [v] Mediterranean couscous

355 Cals

440g WEIGHT   **63g** CARBS

Ingredients 3½

50g **couscous**, uncooked
½ small **red onion** (30g), diced
¼ **green pepper** (25g), diced
⅓ **yellow pepper** (35g), diced
1 small **tomato** (60g), diced
1 tsp **fresh coriander**, chopped
1 clove **garlic**, minced
100g tinned **chickpeas**, drained
½ small **white onion** (35g), diced
½ tsp **dried basil**
½ tsp **paprika**
1 handful **baby spinach** (10g)

16g Prot   **5g** Fat

Preparation

1. Cover the **couscous** with boiling water and leave to stand until the water is absorbed

2. Add the **red onion**, **peppers**, **tomato**, **coriander** and half the **garlic** to a saucepan, and season. Then add 25ml water and cook on a medium heat until the water has reduced slightly (3-4 minutes). Remove from the heat and mix in the couscous

3. In a different pan, add the **chickpeas**, remaining garlic, **white onion**, **basil** and **paprika**. Cook on a medium-high heat for 5 minutes

4. Blend the chickpea mixture in a food processor to form a coarse paste. Shape the mixture into a patty and dry-fry in a non-stick pan for 2-3 minutes on each side

5. Serve on a bed of **baby spinach**, with the couscous

Chicken fajita

385
Cals

300g WEIGHT **46g** CARBS

Preparation

1. Place the **peppers**, **carrot**, **onion**, **tomatoes** and **chicken** in a pan and dry-fry on a medium heat for 1-2 minutes

2. Add the **Cajun seasoning**, **lime juice** and freshly-ground black pepper to taste

3. Pour in 3 tbsp water, cover with a lid and bring to the boil. Reduce the heat and simmer for around 8 minutes, until the chicken is thoroughly cooked

4. Warm the **tortilla** for 1 minute under the grill, or for 10 seconds in a microwave

5. Garnish the fajita mix with **parsley** and serve on a plate with the warmed tortilla

Ingredients 3

½ **red pepper** *(45g), sliced*

½ **green pepper** *(45g), sliced*

30g **carrot**, *sliced lengthways*

½ **red onion** *(45g), sliced*

70g **cherry tomatoes**, *halved*

95g **chicken breast**, *raw with skin removed, sliced*

1 tsp **Cajun seasoning**

2 tsp **lime juice**

1 small **seeded tortilla** *(62g)*

1 tsp **flat-leaf parsley**, *chopped*

32g
Prot

7g
Fat

25 Cals **1**g Prot **0**g Fat

100g WEIGHT **5**g CARBS

Peppers & salsa [v]

Ingredients

⅓ **yellow pepper** *(30g), sliced*
⅓ **orange pepper** *(30g), sliced*
30g **cherry tomatoes**, *chopped*
1 tsp **red onion**, *finely chopped*
1 tsp **lemon juice**

To make the salsa, mix the **tomatoes**, **onion** and **lemon juice**. Season and serve with the **peppers**

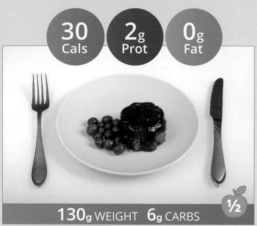

30 Cals **2**g Prot **0**g Fat

130g WEIGHT **6**g CARBS

Berries & jelly

Ingredients

1 *sachet* **sugar-free jelly powder**
40g **strawberries**, *diced*
20g **blueberries**

Make the **jelly** liquid according to pack instructions. Lay the **strawberries** in a small individual mould and pour in 70ml jelly liquid. Place in the fridge to set. Serve with the **blueberries**

30 Cals **2**g Prot **2**g Fat

130g WEIGHT **2**g CARBS

Celery & tzatziki [v]

Ingredients

2 *large* **celery sticks** *(100g)*
30g **tzatziki**

Chop the **celery** into short sticks. Serve with **tzatziki** on the side

Fiery crisps [v]

Ingredients

50g sweet potato, *peeled*
¼ tsp smoked paprika

Pre-heat the oven to 200°C. Using a potato peeler, slice the **potato** into thin strips. Mix the strips with the **paprika** and place on a non-stick oven tray. Cook for 5-7 minutes, shaking half way through. Season and serve

45 Cals **1**g Prot **0**g Fat

20g WEIGHT **11**g CARBS ½

Scallop ceviche

Ingredients

3 scallops (50g), *raw, finely sliced*
½ lime *(zest & juice)*

Mix the **scallops** with the **lime zest and juice**. Leave to stand for at least 5 minutes before serving

45 Cals **8**g Prot **0**g Fat

55g WEIGHT **1**g CARBS

Melon & ham

Ingredients

15g Parma ham
20g gala melon, *sliced*
40g honeydew melon, *sliced*

Slice the **melon** and lay on the **Parma ham** to serve

50 Cals **4**g Prot **2**g Fat

75g WEIGHT **4**g CARBS ½

Vanilla berries [v]

50 Cals   **1**g Prot   **0**g Fat

122g WEIGHT   **11**g CARBS   1½

Ingredients

40g **strawberries**, *quartered*
25g **blueberries**
40g **raspberries**
1 tsp **icing sugar**
⅓ **fresh vanilla pod**
1 tbsp **fresh orange juice**

Place the **fruit** in a bowl. Sprinkle with **icing sugar** & **vanilla pod seeds**. Mix in the **orange juice** and stand for 5 minutes before serving

Olives, feta & veg [v]

50 Cals   **2**g Prot   **3**g Fat

90g WEIGHT   **3**g CARBS   1

Ingredients

25g **cherry tomatoes**, *chopped*
10g **feta cheese**, *in small cubes*
10g **pitted olives** *(in brine), chopped*
1 tsp **lemon juice**
20g **baby corn**, *matchsticked*
20g **carrot**, *matchsticked*

Mix the **tomatoes**, **feta**, **olives** & **lemon juice**. Serve with the **corn** and **carrots** on the side

Prawn kebab

50 Cals   **9**g Prot   **0**g Fat

45g WEIGHT   **2**g CARBS

Ingredients

50g **prawns**, *raw*
25g **pink grapefruit**, *sliced*
½ tsp **Cajun seasoning**

Pre-heat the oven to 200°C. Dust the **prawns** with the **Cajun spices**, salt & pepper. Skewer the **grapefruit** and prawns, and cook on an oven tray for 5-7 minutes

Roast tofu sticks [v]

| **50** Cals | **5**g Prot | **1**g Fat |

Ingredients

60g silken tofu, *matchsticked*
50g cherry tomatoes
½ **red chilli**
1 tsp **lemon juice**
1 *small handful* **basil**
1 tsp **balsamic vinegar**

Pre-heat the oven to 200°C. Cook the **tofu** on a tray for 12 minutes. Mix the **other ingredients** in a food processor. Season and serve

80g WEIGHT   **4**g CARBS

1

Turkey mustard roll

| **60** Cals | **10**g Prot | **1**g Fat |

Ingredients

1 tsp **wholegrain mustard**
45g sliced turkey, *cooked*
20g cherry tomatoes, *quartered*

Spread the **mustard** over one side of the **turkey slice**. Roll into a sausage shape with the mustard on the inside, and cut in half. Serve with the **cherry tomatoes**

68g WEIGHT   **1**g CARBS

Feta & grapes [v]

| **65** Cals | **3**g Prot | **3**g Fat |

Ingredients

15g feta cheese, *cubed*
45g grapes, *halved*

Muddle the cubed **feta** with the **grapes** and serve

60g WEIGHT   **7**g CARBS

½

Yogurt berry crunch [v]

65 Cals **3**g Prot **1**g Fat

Ingredients

45g low-fat natural yogurt
1 small handful **Kellogg's All-bran Golden Crunch** *(5g)*
20g raspberries
20g blueberries

Mix **all the ingredients** together in a bowl and serve

90g WEIGHT **10**g CARBS ½

Avocado salad [v]

70 Cals **1**g Prot **5**g Fat

Ingredients

1 medium **tomato** *(80g), diced*
¼ small **red onion** *(20g), finely diced*
¼ small **avocado** *(25g), diced*
1 tbsp lemon juice
1 small handful **fresh basil**, *roughly torn*

Mix **all the ingredients** together. Season with salt and pepper

143g WEIGHT **5**g CARBS 1½

Celery & nut butter [v]

70 Cals **3**g Prot **6**g Fat

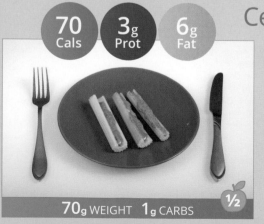

Ingredients

1½ celery sticks *(60g)*
2 tsp almond butter *(10g)*

Chop the **celery** into sticks. Fill with **nut butter** and serve

70g WEIGHT **1**g CARBS ½

Pineapple crispbread [v]

70 Cals **5**g Prot **1**g Fat

Ingredients

1 crispbread (12g)
30g low-fat cottage cheese
25g pineapple chunks

Spread the **crispbread** with **cottage cheese** and top with the **pineapple** chunks

62g WEIGHT   **12**g CARBS

Mozzarella & tomato [v]

70 Cals **5**g Prot **5**g Fat

Ingredients

2 fresh basil leaves
25g buffalo mozzarella, sliced
½ small **tomato** (35g), sliced

Lay the **basil leaves** on the **mozzarella**. Top with the slices of **tomato** and serve

61g WEIGHT   **1**g CARBS

Tomato bruschetta [v]

70 Cals **2**g Prot **1**g Fat

Ingredients

2 thin slices **baguette** (20g)
½ medium **tomato** (50g), diced
¼ small **red onion** (20g), finely diced
1 small handful **fresh basil**, torn

Pre-heat the oven to 200°C. Cook the **bread** on a baking sheet for 3 minutes. Mix the **tomato**, **onion** and **basil**. Season with salt and pepper. Top the toasted bread with the tomato and onion mix

80g WEIGHT   **15**g CARBS

Parmesan tomatoes [v]

75 Cals **4**g Prot **2**g Fat

125g WEIGHT **12g** CARBS

Ingredients

*½ tsp dried **oregano***
*5g **parmesan**, grated*
*10g **breadcrumbs***
*1½ medium **tomatoes** (120g), halved*

Pre-heat the oven to 200°C. Mix the **oregano** and **parmesan** into the **breadcrumbs**. Coat the **tomatoes** in breadcrumbs, placing any extra on top. Bake for 10 minutes until the breadcrumbs have turned golden

Mango prawns

75 Cals **11**g Prot **1**g Fat

75g WEIGHT **6g** CARBS

Ingredients

*50g **prawns**, cooked*
*15g **mango**, in small cubes*
*2 tsp **sweet chilli sauce** (10g)*

Stir together the **prawns** and **mango**. Serve with the **sweet chilli sauce** on the side

Squash & feta salad [v]

75 Cals **4**g Prot **4**g Fat

100g WEIGHT **6g** CARBS

Ingredients

*⅛ **butternut squash** (60g), cubed with skin on*
*20g **feta cheese**, cubed*
*¼ **yellow peppers** (20g), diced*
*¼ tsp **chilli flakes***

Pre-heat the oven to 200°C. Roast the **squash** for 25-30 minutes. Mix with the **feta** and **peppers**. Add **chilli flakes** to taste, and serve

Yogurt & strawberries [v]

75 Cals **6**g Prot **1**g Fat

Ingredients

100g *low-fat natural yogurt*
50g *strawberries*, quartered
1 *small handful* **mint leaves**, roughly torn

Stir together **all the ingredients** and serve

153g WEIGHT   **10**g CARBS ½

Veg & houmous [v]

80 Cals **5**g Prot **4**g Fat

Ingredients

45g *baby corn*
45g *mangetout*
2 tbsp *houmous* (30g)

Top and tail the **vegetables**, and serve with **houmous** on the side

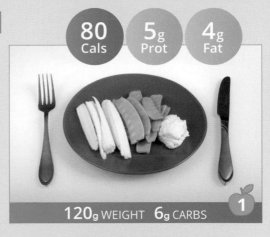

120g WEIGHT   **6**g CARBS 1

Baked squash seeds [v]

80 Cals **5**g Prot **6**g Fat

Ingredients

15g *butternut squash (or pumpkin) seeds*
½ tsp *paprika*

Pre-heat the oven to 200°C. Remove **seeds** from a butternut squash. Lay the seeds on a baking tray and sprinkle with the **paprika**. Add freshly ground salt and pepper to taste. Cook for 8-10 minutes

15g WEIGHT   **2**g CARBS

Garlic corn cob [v]

85 Cals   **3**g Prot   **2**g Fat

128g WEIGHT   **15**g CARBS   ½

Ingredients

½ *large* **corn on the cob** *(125g)*
½ *clove* **garlic**, *minced*

Pre-heat the oven to 200°C. Bring a pan of water to the boil and cook the **corn** for 10 minutes. Place the cooked corn in foil. Rub over the **garlic**, and season. Oven cook for 15 minutes

Mango on ice [v]

85 Cals   **1**g Prot   **0**g Fat

122g WEIGHT   **21**g CARBS   1

Ingredients

1 *handful fresh* **mint leaves**, *roughly torn*
80g **mango**, *diced*
40g **mango sorbet** *(1 scoop)*

Sprinkle the **mint** over the **mango**. Top with the **sorbet** and serve

Banana rice cake [v]

85 Cals   **2**g Prot   **3**g Fat

34g WEIGHT   **12**g CARBS

Ingredients

1 **wholegrain rice cake** *(9g)*
1 tsp **almond butter** *(5g)*
⅓ **banana** *(20g), sliced*

Spread the **rice cake** with the **almond butter**. Top with slices of **banana** and serve

5-spice popcorn [v]

90 Cals | **2g** Prot | **5g** Fat

20g WEIGHT **10g** CARBS

Ingredients

15g corn kernels, *raw*
1 tsp coconut oil
1 tsp Chinese 5-spice

Add the **kernels** to a lidded non-stick pan on medium heat. After 3 minutes the corn will pop. Reduce the heat and agitate the pan. Once all the corn has popped, remove from the heat. Add the **oil** and **spice**, shake and serve

Prunes in ham

90 Cals | **6g** Prot | **3g** Fat

50g WEIGHT **10g** CARBS

Ingredients

3-4 prunes *(30g),*
  halved & destoned
2 *slices* **serrano ham** *(20g)*

Place the **prunes** on the **ham** and roll to make a sausage shape

Tuna crunch

90 Cals | **13g** Prot | **1g** Fat

130g WEIGHT **9g** CARBS

Ingredients

50g tuna *(tinned in water),*
  drained
30g *tinned* **sweetcorn**
1 celery stick *(35g), sliced*
2 tsp lemon juice

Mix **all the ingredients** in a bowl. Season with salt and pepper

49 Cals **1**g Prot **2**g Fat

Chocolate Chip Cookie
10g Weight   6g Carbs

44 Cals **1**g Prot **1**g Fat

Ginger Biscuit
10g Weight   8g Carbs

49 Cals **1**g Prot **1**g Fat

Jaffa Cake
13g Weight   10g Carbs

40 Cals **1**g Prot **2**g Fat

Malted Milk
8g Weight   5g Carbs

26 Cals **0**g Prot **1**g Fat

Milk Chocolate Finger
5g Weight   3g Carbs

40 Cals **1**g Prot **2**g Fat

Nice Biscuit
8g Weight   5g Carbs

31 Cals | **1**g Prot | **1**g Fat

Rich Tea
7g Weight 5g Carbs

50 Cals | **1**g Prot | **3**g Fat

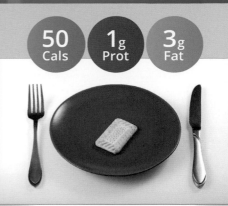

Shortcake
10g Weight 6g Carbs

20 Cals | **1**g Prot | **0**g Fat

Breadstick
5g Weight 4g Carbs

26 Cals | **1**g Prot | **2**g Fat

Cheddar
5g Weight 3g Carbs

35 Cals | **1**g Prot | **2**g Fat

Cheese Straw
7g Weight 3g Carbs

33 Cals | **1**g Prot | **1**g Fat

Cream Cracker
8g Weight 6g Carbs

34 Cals   **1**g Prot   **0**g Fat

Crispbread
11g Weight   8g Carbs

45 Cals   **1**g Prot   **2**g Fat

Oatcake
10g Weight   6g Carbs

47 Cals   **1**g Prot   **3**g Fat

Puffed Cracker
9g Weight   5g Carbs

30 Cals   **1**g Prot   **0**g Fat

Rice Cake
8g Weight   7g Carbs

26 Cals   **1**g Prot   **1**g Fat

Water Biscuit
6g Weight   5g Carbs

33 Cals   **1**g Prot   **1**g Fat

Wholegrain Cracker
8g Weight   6g Carbs

78 Cals | **3**g Prot | **1**g Fat

Granary Bread
33g Weight (medium slice)   16g Carbs

104 Cals | **4**g Prot | **1**g Fat

Granary Bread
44g Weight (thick slice)   21g Carbs

72 Cals | **3**g Prot | **1**g Fat

White Bread
33g Weight (medium slice)   15g Carbs

96 Cals | **4**g Prot | **1**g Fat

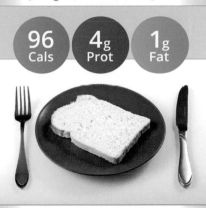

White Bread
44g Weight (thick slice)   20g Carbs

122 Cals | **5**g Prot | **1**g Fat

Bap (white)
48g Weight   25g Carbs

124 Cals | **5**g Prot | **2**g Fat

Bap (wholemeal)
51g Weight   24g Carbs

79 Cals **3**g Prot **1**g Fat

Baguette
30g Weight   17g Carbs

86 Cals **3**g Prot **0**g Fat

Crumpet
45g Weight   17g Carbs

66 Cals **2**g Prot **2**g Fat

Croutons
15g Weight   10g Carbs

104 Cals **4**g Prot **1**g Fat

Finger Roll
41g Weight   21g Carbs

76 Cals **2**g Prot **3**g Fat

Garlic Bread
22g Weight   10g Carbs

158 Cals **6**g Prot **1**g Fat

Rye Bread
72g Weight   33g Carbs

147 Cals   **7**g Prot   **1**g Fat

Pitta Bread *(wholemeal)*
60g Weight   27g Carbs

177 Cals   **6**g Prot   **3**g Fat

Tortilla *(wholemeal)*
65g Weight   29g Carbs

77 Cals   **1**g Prot   **4**g Fat

Taco Shell
15g Weight   9g Carbs

65 Cals   **2**g Prot   **5**g Fat

Poppadom
13g Weight (small)   4g Carbs

182 Cals   **7**g Prot   **1**g Fat

Chapati *(without fat)*
90g Weight   39g Carbs

94 Cals   **4**g Prot   **1**g Fat

Roti
43g Weight   20g Carbs

64 Cals **1**g Prot **2**g Fat

Brioche
18g Weight   9g Carbs

157 Cals **3**g Prot **6**g Fat

Granola
35g Weight   22g Carbs

97 Cals **2**g Prot **5**g Fat

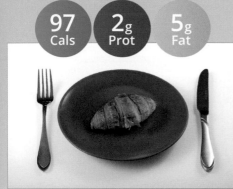

Mini Croissant
26g Weight   11g Carbs

109 Cals **3**g Prot **2**g Fat

Muesli
30g Weight   22g Carbs

142 Cals **3**g Prot **8**g Fat

Mini Pain au Chocolat
32g Weight   15g Carbs

110 Cals **3**g Prot **2**g Fat

Muesli *(no added sugar)*
30g Weight   20g Carbs

54 Cals **3**g Prot **1**g Fat

All Bran
20g Weight   9g Carbs

108 Cals **5**g Prot **2**g Fat

All Bran
40g Weight   18g Carbs

50 Cals **2**g Prot **0**g Fat

Bran Flakes
15g Weight   11g Carbs

99 Cals **3**g Prot **1**g Fat

Bran Flakes
30g Weight   21g Carbs

56 Cals **1**g Prot **0**g Fat

Corn Flakes
15g Weight   13g Carbs

113 Cals **2**g Prot **0**g Fat

Corn Flakes
30g Weight   27g Carbs

71 Cals **2**g Prot **1**g Fat

Fruit & Fibre
20g Weight   15g Carbs

141 Cals **4**g Prot **2**g Fat

Fruit & Fibre
40g Weight   29g Carbs

61 Cals **1**g Prot **1**g Fat

Honey Nut Flakes
15g Weight   14g Carbs

122 Cals **2**g Prot **1**g Fat

Honey Nut Flakes
30g Weight   27g Carbs

48 Cals **1**g Prot **0**g Fat

Malted Wheats
14g Weight   11g Carbs

145 Cals **4**g Prot **1**g Fat

Malted Wheats
42g Weight   33g Carbs

55 Cals **1**g Prot **1**g Fat

Multigrain Hoops
15g Weight 12g Carbs

110 Cals **2**g Prot **1**g Fat

Multigrain Hoops
30g Weight 24g Carbs

74 Cals **2**g Prot **0**g Fat

Raisin Bites
22g Weight 17g Carbs

152 Cals **4**g Prot **1**g Fat

Raisin Bites
45g Weight 34g Carbs

38 Cals **1**g Prot **0**g Fat

Rice Snaps
10g Weight 9g Carbs

76 Cals **1**g Prot **0**g Fat

Rice Snaps
20g Weight 19g Carbs

57 Cals **2**g Prot **0**g Fat

Special Flakes with Berries
15g Weight   12g Carbs

114 Cals **4**g Prot **1**g Fat

Special Flakes with Berries
30g Weight   23g Carbs

84 Cals **4**g Prot **2**g Fat

Porridge *(made with semi-skimmed milk)*
75g Weight   11g Carbs

246 Cals **13**g Prot **7**g Fat

Porridge *(made with semi-skimmed milk)*
220g Weight   33g Carbs

35 Cals **1**g Prot **1**g Fat

Porridge *(made with water)*
75g Weight   6g Carbs

101 Cals **3**g Prot **2**g Fat

Porridge *(made with water)*
220g Weight   18g Carbs

72 Cals **2**g Prot **0**g Fat

Oat Biscuit
20g Weight   14g Carbs

66 Cals **3**g Prot **4**g Fat

Milk *(whole)*
100ml   5g Carbs

67 Cals **2**g Prot **1**g Fat

Wheat Biscuit
19g Weight   14g Carbs

46 Cals **3**g Prot **2**g Fat

Milk *(semi-skimmed)*
100ml   5g Carbs

73 Cals **3**g Prot **0**g Fat

Wheat Pillow
22g Weight   16g Carbs

32 Cals **3**g Prot **0**g Fat

Milk *(skimmed)*
100ml   4g Carbs

136 Cals **3**g Prot **7**g Fat

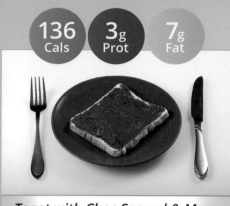

Toast with Choc Spread & Marg
36g Weight (5g marg, 5g choc) 18g Carbs

124 Cals **3**g Prot **5**g Fat

Toast with Honey & Margarine
36g Weight (5g marg, 5g honey) 19g Carbs

122 Cals **3**g Prot **5**g Fat

Toast with Jam & Margarine
36g Weight (5g marg, 5g jam) 18g Carbs

124 Cals **3**g Prot **5**g Fat

Toast with Lemon Curd & Marg
36g Weight (5g marg, 5g lemon) 18g Carbs

123 Cals **3**g Prot **5**g Fat

Toast with Marmalade & Marg
36g Weight (5g marg, 5g marm) 19g Carbs

140 Cals **4**g Prot **7**g Fat

Toast with Peanut Butter & Marg
36g Weight (5g marg, 5g peanut) 16g Carbs

89 Cals | **1**g Prot | **3**g Fat

Fruit Cake
26g Weight   16g Carbs

109 Cals | **1**g Prot | **3**g Fat

Ginger Cake
30g Weight   19g Carbs

89 Cals | **2**g Prot | **1**g Fat

Malt Loaf
30g Weight   20g Carbs

120 Cals | **3**g Prot | **3**g Fat

Fruit Scone
38g Weight   21g Carbs

159 Cals | **4**g Prot | **4**g Fat

Hot Cross Bun
51g Weight   30g Carbs

123 Cals | **2**g Prot | **3**g Fat

Iced Bun
37g Weight   21g Carbs

120 Cals   **1**g Prot   **3**g Fat

Mini Battenburg
30g Weight   21g Carbs

45 Cals   **1**g Prot   **2**g Fat

Mini Doughnut
11g Weight   6g Carbs

138 Cals   **2**g Prot   **6**g Fat

Swiss Roll
35g Weight   20g Carbs

167 Cals   **2**g Prot   **6**g Fat

Mince Pie
42g Weight   26g Carbs

96 Cals   **1**g Prot   **5**g Fat

Mini Blueberry Muffin
25g Weight   11g Carbs

108 Cals   **2**g Prot   **5**g Fat

Mini Chocolate Muffin
28g Weight   15g Carbs

86 Cals   **5**g Prot   **7**g Fat

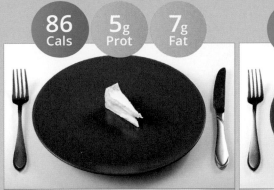

Brie
25g Weight   0g Carbs

73 Cals   **5**g Prot   **6**g Fat

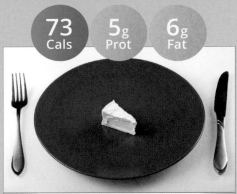

Camembert
25g Weight   0g Carbs

104 Cals   **6**g Prot   **9**g Fat

Cheddar
25g Weight   0g Carbs

104 Cals   **6**g Prot   **9**g Fat

Cheddar (grated)
25g Weight   0g Carbs

68 Cals   **8**g Prot   **4**g Fat

Cheddar (reduced fat)
25g Weight   0g Carbs

51 Cals   **6**g Prot   **2**g Fat

Cottage Cheese
50g Weight   2g Carbs

62 Cals **1**g Prot **6**g Fat

85 Cals **7**g Prot **7**g Fat

Cream Cheese
25g Weight   1g Carbs

Edam
25g Weight   0g Carbs

63 Cals **4**g Prot **5**g Fat

80 Cals **5**g Prot **7**g Fat

Feta
25g Weight   0g Carbs

Goat's Cheese
25g Weight   0g Carbs

80 Cals **5**g Prot **6**g Fat

64 Cals **5**g Prot **5**g Fat

Halloumi
25g Weight   1g Carbs

Mozzarella
25g Weight   0g Carbs

42 Cals **4**g Prot **3**g Fat

Parmesan *(grated)*
10g Weight   0g Carbs

59 Cals **4**g Prot **5**g Fat

Processed Cheese Slice
20g Weight   1g Carbs

48 Cals **2**g Prot **4**g Fat

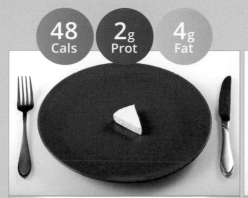

Spreadable Cheese
18g Weight   1g Carbs

103 Cals **6**g Prot **9**g Fat

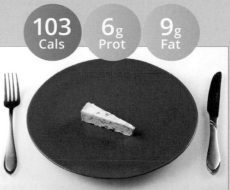

Stilton
25g Weight   0g Carbs

100 Cals **6**g Prot **8**g Fat

Red Leicester
25g Weight   0g Carbs

94 Cals **5**g Prot **7**g Fat

Wensleydale with Cranberries
25g Weight   3g Carbs

95 Cals | **1**g Prot | **6**g Fat

Crisps
18g Weight   10g Carbs

83 Cals | **1**g Prot | **5**g Fat

Chocolate (milk)
16g Weight   9g Carbs

50 Cals | **1**g Prot | **1**g Fat

Pretzels
13g Weight   10g Carbs

82 Cals | **1**g Prot | **5**g Fat

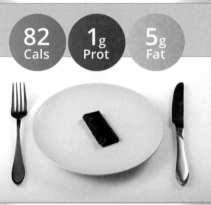

Chocolate (dark)
16g Weight   10g Carbs

73 Cals | **1**g Prot | **4**g Fat

Tortilla Chips
16g Weight   10g Carbs

91 Cals | **1**g Prot | **5**g Fat

Chocolate Honeycomb Balls
18g Weight   11g Carbs

120 Cals **1**g Prot **4**g Fat

Apple & Rhubarb Crumble
60g Weight   20g Carbs

109 Cals **1**g Prot **5**g Fat

Apple Strudel
45g Weight   15g Carbs

148 Cals **1**g Prot **9**g Fat

Banoffee Pie
43g Weight   16g Carbs

141 Cals **2**g Prot **10**g Fat

Chocolate Torte
33g Weight   10g Carbs

147 Cals **2**g Prot **8**g Fat

Cheesecake
50g Weight   18g Carbs

57 Cals **2**g Prot **1**g Fat

Custard (made with semi-skimmed milk)
60g Weight   10g Carbs

71 Cals **1**g Prot **4**g Fat

52 Cals **1**g Prot **0**g Fat

Ice Cream *(vanilla)*
40g Weight   8g Carbs

Jelly
85g Weight   13g Carbs

5 Cals **1**g Prot **0**g Fat

110 Cals **1**g Prot **4**g Fat

Jelly *(sugar-free)*
85g Weight   0g Carbs

Lemon Meringue Pie
44g Weight   19g Carbs

75 Cals **2**g Prot **3**g Fat

138 Cals **2**g Prot **10**g Fat

Mousse *(chocolate)*
50g Weight   10g Carbs

Profiteroles
40g Weight   10g Carbs

119 Cals   **5**g Prot   **2**g Fat

Rice Pudding
140g Weight   23g Carbs

52 Cals   **0**g Prot   **0**g Fat

Sorbet *(raspberry)*
45g Weight   11g Carbs

58 Cals   **2**g Prot   **2**g Fat

Strawberry Delight
50g Weight   8g Carbs

133 Cals   **4**g Prot   **1**g Fat

Summer Pudding
140g Weight   30g Carbs

1

115 Cals   **2**g Prot   **5**g Fat

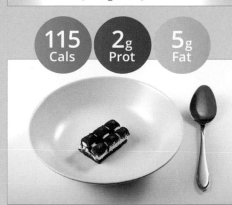

Tiramisu
45g Weight   15g Carbs

87 Cals   **1**g Prot   **4**g Fat

Trifle
55g Weight   11g Carbs

57 Cals **0**g Prot **0**g Fat

Apple Juice
150ml   15g Carbs
1

92 Cals **0**g Prot **0**g Fat

Cranberry Juice
150ml   22g Carbs
1

50 Cals **1**g Prot **0**g Fat

Grapefruit Juice
150ml   12g Carbs
1

54 Cals **1**g Prot **0**g Fat

Orange Juice
150ml   13g Carbs
1

62 Cals **0**g Prot **0**g Fat

Pineapple Juice
150ml   16g Carbs
1

21 Cals **1**g Prot **0**g Fat

Tomato Juice
150ml   5g Carbs
1

62 Cals   **0**g Prot   **0**g Fat

2 Cals   **0**g Prot   **0**g Fat

Cola
150ml   16g Carbs

Diet Cola
150ml   0g Carbs

39 Cals   **0**g Prot   **0**g Fat

78 Cals   **1**g Prot   **0**g Fat

Iced Tea
150ml   10g Carbs

Smoothie (strawberry & banana)
150ml   18g Carbs   1

68 Cals   **0**g Prot   **0**g Fat

6 Cals   **0**g Prot   **0**g Fat

Squash
150ml   18g Carbs

Squash (no added sugar)
150ml   1g Carbs

1 Cals **0**g Prot **0**g Fat

Espresso
60ml   0g Carbs

55 Cals **5**g Prot **0**g Fat

Cappuccino (skimmed milk)
235ml (small, 8 fl oz)   8g Carbs

18 Cals **2**g Prot **1**g Fat

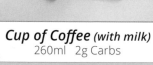

Cup of Coffee (with milk)
260ml   2g Carbs

67 Cals **6**g Prot **0**g Fat

Latte (skimmed milk)
235ml (small, 8 fl oz)   10g Carbs

18 Cals **1**g Prot **1**g Fat

Cup of Tea (with milk)
260ml   2g Carbs

141 Cals **8**g Prot **2**g Fat

Hot Chocolate (skimmed milk)
235ml (small, 8 fl oz)   25g Carbs

94 Cals **0**g Prot **0**g Fat

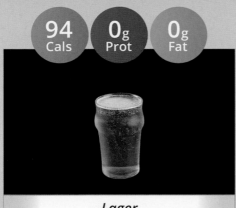

Lager
284ml (half pint)   4g Carbs

85 Cals **1**g Prot **0**g Fat

Stout
284ml (half pint)   4g Carbs

119 Cals **0**g Prot **0**g Fat

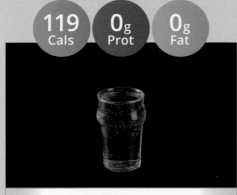

Cider *(sweet)*
284ml (half pint)   12g Carbs

56 Cals **0**g Prot **0**g Fat

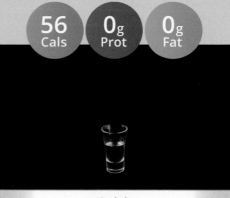

Spirit
25ml   0g Carbs

85 Cals **0**g Prot **0**g Fat

Red Wine
125ml (small glass)   0g Carbs

83 Cals **0**g Prot **0**g Fat

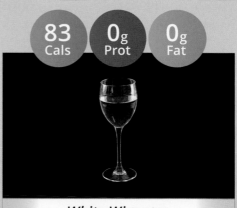

White Wine *(dry)*
125ml (small glass)   1g Carbs

88 Cals **8**g Prot **6**g Fat

Boiled Egg
60g Weight   0g Carbs

90 Cals **7**g Prot **7**g Fat

Fried Egg
50g Weight   0g Carbs

74 Cals **6**g Prot **5**g Fat

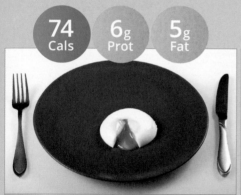

Poached Egg
50g Weight   0g Carbs

109 Cals **9**g Prot **8**g Fat

Scrambled Egg (with milk)
70g Weight (1 egg)   1g Carbs

98 Cals **6**g Prot **8**g Fat

Omelette (plain)
50g Weight (1 egg)   0g Carbs

195 Cals **11**g Prot **17**g Fat

Omelette (plain)
100g Weight (2 eggs)   0g Carbs

139 Cals **9**g Prot **4**g Fat

Fish Cake *(baked)*
90g Weight   18g Carbs

40 Cals **3**g Prot **2**g Fat

Fish Finger *(baked)*
20g Weight   3g Carbs

166 Cals **7**g Prot **10**g Fat

Scampi *(fried)*
70g Weight   14g Carbs

215 Cals **14**g Prot **9**g Fat

Fish *(breaded, baked)*
106g Weight   20g Carbs

50 Cals **11**g Prot **1**g Fat

Prawns *(boiled)*
50g Weight   0g Carbs

99 Cals **23**g Prot **1**g Fat

Prawns *(boiled)*
100g Weight   0g Carbs

50 Cals   **11**g Prot   **1**g Fat   **99** Cals   **23**g Prot   **1**g Fat

King Prawns *(boiled)*
50g Weight   0g Carbs

King Prawns *(boiled)*
100g Weight   0g Carbs

142 Cals   **18**g Prot   **8**g Fat   **69** Cals   **17**g Prot   **0**g Fat

Salmon *(tinned in brine)*
85g Weight (half tin)   0g Carbs

Tuna *(tinned in brine)*
70g Weight (half tin)   0g Carbs

86 Cals   **11**g Prot   **5**g Fat   **81** Cals   **9**g Prot   **5**g Fat

Sardines *(in brine)*
50g Weight (half tin)   0g Carbs

Sardines *(in tomato sauce)*
50g Weight (half tin)   1g Carbs

266 Cals **14**g Prot **23**g Fat

Smoked Mackerel
75g Weight   0g Carbs

71 Cals **13**g Prot **2**g Fat

Smoked Salmon
50g Weight   0g Carbs

68 Cals **14**g Prot **1**g Fat

Saltfish *(boiled)*
80g Weight   0g Carbs

120 Cals **27**g Prot **2**g Fat

Cod / Haddock *(baked)*
125g Weight   0g Carbs

139 Cals **29**g Prot **2**g Fat

Plaice *(grilled)*
145g Weight   0g Carbs

65 Cals **12**g Prot **2**g Fat

Scallops *(fried)*
50g Weight   0g Carbs

280 Cals   **32**g Prot   **17**g Fat

Salmon Steak *(grilled)*
130g Weight   0g Carbs

177 Cals   **31**g Prot   **6**g Fat

Tuna Steak *(grilled)*
130g Weight   0g Carbs

142 Cals   **23**g Prot   **6**g Fat

Trout Fillet *(grilled)*
105g Weight   0g Carbs

45 Cals   **10**g Prot   **0**g Fat

Crab Meat
60g Weight   1g Carbs

87 Cals   **5**g Prot   **1**g Fat

Seafood Sticks
80g Weight   14g Carbs

59 Cals   **3**g Prot   **3**g Fat

Calamari *(fried)*
30g Weight   5g Carbs

38 Cals **2**g Prot **2**g Fat

Prawn Tempura
15g Weight   2g Carbs

50 Cals **1**g Prot **1**g Fat

California Roll
35g Weight   9g Carbs

40 Cals **1**g Prot **1**g Fat

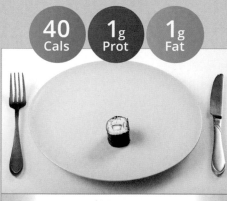

Maki *(Prawn)*
24g Weight   7g Carbs

54 Cals **2**g Prot **2**g Fat

Nigiri *(Salmon)*
34g Weight   8g Carbs

40 Cals **3**g Prot **0**g Fat

Nigiri *(Tuna)*
28g Weight   7g Carbs

27 Cals **3**g Prot **2**g Fat

Sashimi *(Salmon)*
15g Weight   0g Carbs

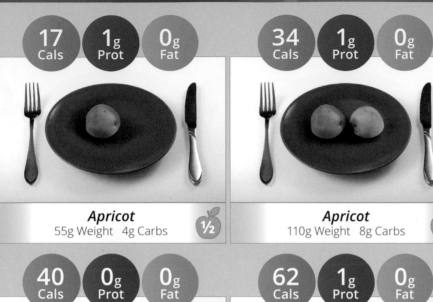

17 Cals   **1**g Prot   **0**g Fat

Apricot
55g Weight   4g Carbs   ½

34 Cals   **1**g Prot   **0**g Fat

Apricot
110g Weight   8g Carbs   1

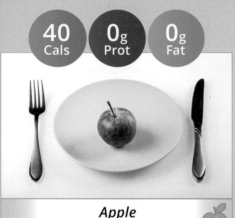

40 Cals   **0**g Prot   **0**g Fat

Apple
85g Weight   10g Carbs   1

62 Cals   **1**g Prot   **0**g Fat

Apple
131g Weight   16g Carbs   1

10 Cals   **0**g Prot   **0**g Fat

Blackberries
40g Weight   2g Carbs   ½

20 Cals   **1**g Prot   **0**g Fat

Blackberries
80g Weight   4g Carbs   1

60 Cals **1**g Prot **0**g Fat

Banana
97g Weight   15g Carbs   ½

81 Cals **1**g Prot **0**g Fat

Banana
130g Weight   20g Carbs   1

26 Cals **0**g Prot **0**g Fat

Blueberries
40g Weight   6g Carbs   ½

53 Cals **1**g Prot **0**g Fat

Blueberries
80g Weight   11g Carbs   1

24 Cals **1**g Prot **0**g Fat

Cherries
50g Weight   6g Carbs   ½

48 Cals **1**g Prot **0**g Fat

Cherries
100g Weight   12g Carbs   1

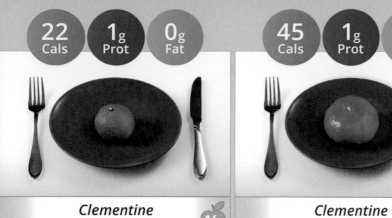

| **22** Cals | **1**g Prot | **0**g Fat | | **45** Cals | **1**g Prot | **0**g Fat |

Clementine
80g Weight   5g Carbs   ½

Clementine
160g Weight   10g Carbs   1

| **13** Cals | **0**g Prot | **0**g Fat | | **24** Cals | **1**g Prot | **0**g Fat |

Figs
30g Weight   3g Carbs

Figs
55g Weight   5g Carbs   ½

| **46** Cals | **1**g Prot | **0**g Fat | | **46** Cals | **1**g Prot | **0**g Fat |

Grapefruit
228g Weight   11g Carbs   1

Grapefruit
140g Weight (1 grapefruit)   11g Carbs   1

48 Cals **0**g Prot **0**g Fat

Grapes *(seedless)*
80g Weight   12g Carbs

96 Cals **1**g Prot **0**g Fat

Grapes *(seedless)*
160g Weight   25g Carbs

23 Cals **1**g Prot **0**g Fat

Kiwi
55g Weight   5g Carbs

25 Cals **1**g Prot **0**g Fat

Kiwi
51g Weight (1 kiwi)   5g Carbs

46 Cals **1**g Prot **0**g Fat

Mango
80g Weight   11g Carbs

91 Cals **1**g Prot **0**g Fat

Mango
160g Weight   23g Carbs

| 22 Cals | 1g Prot | 0g Fat |

Melon *(honeydew)*
80g Weight   5g Carbs   **1**

| 45 Cals | 1g Prot | 0g Fat |

Melon *(honeydew)*
160g Weight   11g Carbs   **1**

| 19 Cals | 1g Prot | 0g Fat |

Orange
71g Weight   4g Carbs   **½**

| 30 Cals | 1g Prot | 0g Fat |

Orange
115g Weight   7g Carbs   **1**

| 22 Cals | 1g Prot | 0g Fat |

Papaya
80g Weight   4g Carbs   **1**

| 43 Cals | 1g Prot | 0g Fat |

Papaya
160g Weight   9g Carbs   **1**

20 Cals   **1**g Prot   **0**g Fat

Pomegranate
40g Weight   5g Carbs   ½

41 Cals   **1**g Prot   **0**g Fat

Pomegranate
80g Weight   9g Carbs   1

20 Cals   **0**g Prot   **0**g Fat

Plum
55g Weight   5g Carbs   ½

40 Cals   **1**g Prot   **0**g Fat

Plum
110g Weight   10g Carbs   1

66 Cals   **2**g Prot   **0**g Fat

Nectarine
165g Weight   15g Carbs   1

46 Cals   **1**g Prot   **0**g Fat

Peach
138g Weight   11g Carbs   1

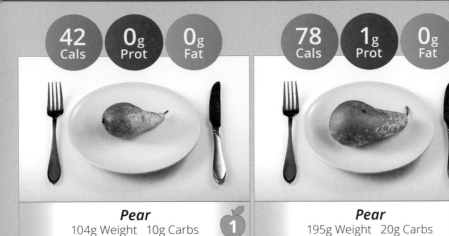

42 Cals **0g** Prot **0g** Fat

78 Cals **1g** Prot **0g** Fat

Pear
104g Weight   10g Carbs   **1**

Pear
195g Weight   20g Carbs   **1**

16 Cals **0g** Prot **0g** Fat

33 Cals **0g** Prot **0g** Fat

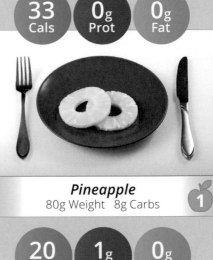

Pineapple
40g Weight   4g Carbs   **½**

Pineapple
80g Weight   8g Carbs   **1**

10 Cals **1g** Prot **0g** Fat

20 Cals **1g** Prot **0g** Fat

Raspberries
40g Weight   2g Carbs   **½**

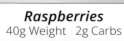

Raspberries
80g Weight   4g Carbs   **1**

38 Cals **1**g Prot **0**g Fat

Rhubarb *(stewed)*
80g Weight   9g Carbs

77 Cals **1**g Prot **0**g Fat

Rhubarb *(stewed)*
160g Weight   18g Carbs

22 Cals **1**g Prot **0**g Fat

Strawberries
80g Weight   5g Carbs

38 Cals **1**g Prot **0**g Fat

Strawberries
140g Weight   8g Carbs

25 Cals **0**g Prot **0**g Fat

Watermelon
80g Weight   6g Carbs

43 Cals **1**g Prot **0**g Fat

Watermelon
140g Weight   10g Carbs

36 Cals   **0**g Prot   **0**g Fat

Apple Rings   ½
15g Weight   9g Carbs

56 Cals   **1**g Prot   **0**g Fat

Apricot
30g Weight   13g Carbs

103 Cals   **0**g Prot   **0**g Fat

Cranberries
30g Weight   25g Carbs

81 Cals   **1**g Prot   **0**g Fat

Dates   1
30g Weight   20g Carbs

68 Cals   **1**g Prot   **1**g Fat

Figs   1
30g Weight   16g Carbs

83 Cals   **1**g Prot   **0**g Fat

Pineapple
30g Weight   20g Carbs

48 Cals   **1**g Prot   **0**g Fat

Prunes
30g Weight   10g Carbs

96 Cals   **2**g Prot   **0**g Fat

Prunes
60g Weight   21g Carbs

32 Cals   **0**g Prot   **0**g Fat

Raisins
11g Weight (tablespoon)   8g Carbs

87 Cals   **1**g Prot   **0**g Fat

Raisins
30g Weight   21g Carbs

38 Cals   **0**g Prot   **0**g Fat

Sultanas
13g Weight (tablespoon)   9g Carbs

88 Cals   **1**g Prot   **0**g Fat

Sultanas
30g Weight   21g Carbs

8 Cals **1**g Prot **0**g Fat

Gherkins ½
55g Weight   1g Carbs

26 Cals **0**g Prot **3**g Fat

Olives (pitted, in brine)
25g Weight   0g Carbs

65 Cals **1**g Prot **4**g Fat

Onion Rings (battered)
26g Weight   7g Carbs

8 Cals **0**g Prot **0**g Fat

Pickled Onions
35g Weight   2g Carbs

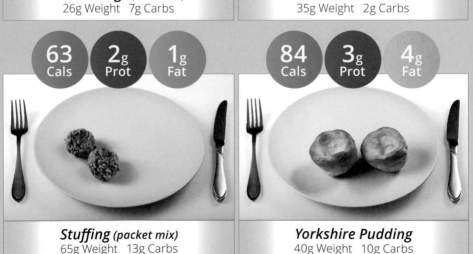

63 Cals **2**g Prot **1**g Fat

Stuffing (packet mix)
65g Weight   13g Carbs

84 Cals **3**g Prot **4**g Fat

Yorkshire Pudding
40g Weight   10g Carbs

52 Cals   **4**g Prot   **4**g Fat

30 Cals   **2**g Prot   **2**g Fat

Back Bacon *(grilled)*
18g Weight   0g Carbs

Streaky Bacon *(grilled)*
9g Weight   0g Carbs

17 Cals   **1**g Prot   **1**g Fat

20 Cals   **1**g Prot   **2**g Fat

Chorizo
6g Weight   0g Carbs

Pancetta *(dry fried)*
5g Weight   0g Carbs

37 Cals   **4**g Prot   **2**g Fat

162 Cals   **8**g Prot   **12**g Fat

Parma Ham
15g Weight   0g Carbs

Sausage *(grilled)*
55g Weight   5g Carbs

69 Cals **13**g Prot **2**g Fat

Beef Slice
50g Weight   0g Carbs

16 Cals **2**g Prot **1**g Fat

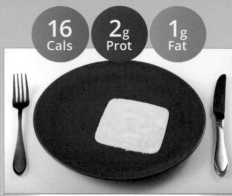

Wafer-thin Chicken
12g Weight   1g Carbs

32 Cals **6**g Prot **1**g Fat

Ham Slice
30g Weight   0g Carbs

13 Cals **2**g Prot **0**g Fat

Wafer-thin Ham
12g Weight   0g Carbs

49 Cals **9**g Prot **1**g Fat

Turkey Slice
40g Weight   0g Carbs

8 Cals **1**g Prot **0**g Fat

Wafer-thin Turkey
8g Weight   0g Carbs

169 Cals **23**g Prot **8**g Fat

Gammon *(grilled)*
85g Weight   0g Carbs

96 Cals **11**g Prot **6**g Fat

Roast Lamb
40g Weight   0g Carbs

175 Cals **20**g Prot **11**g Fat

Pork Chop *(grilled)*
68g Weight   0g Carbs

161 Cals **23**g Prot **8**g Fat

Roast Pork
75g Weight   0g Carbs

115 Cals **25**g Prot **2**g Fat

Roast Turkey *(with skin)*
75g Weight   0g Carbs

132 Cals **30**g Prot **1**g Fat

Turkey Breast *(grilled)*
85g Weight   0g Carbs

139 Cals **19**g Prot **7**g Fat

Chicken Drumstick (roasted)
75g Weight   0g Carbs

155 Cals **19**g Prot **9**g Fat

Rump Steak (fried)
68g Weight   0g Carbs

141 Cals **30**g Prot **2**g Fat

Chicken Breast (grilled, without skin)
95g Weight   0g Carbs

225 Cals **24**g Prot **14**g Fat

Sirloin Steak (fried)
112g Weight   0g Carbs

106 Cals **16**g Prot **5**g Fat

Roast Chicken (with skin)
60g Weight   0g Carbs

167 Cals **22**g Prot **9**g Fat

Roast Beef
75g Weight   0g Carbs

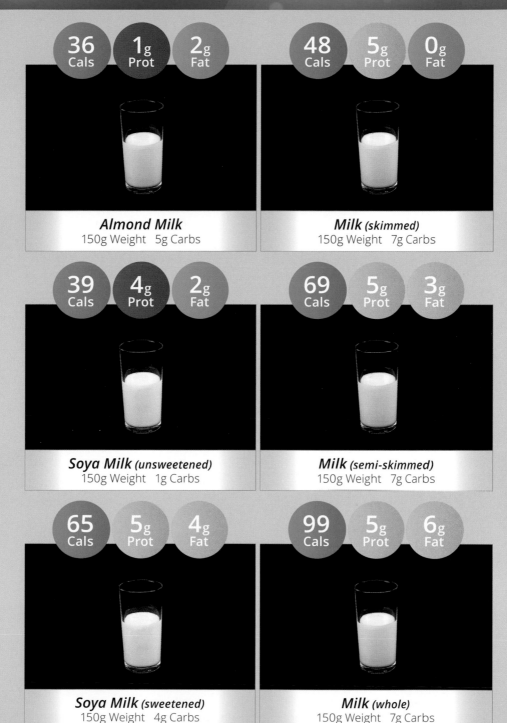

36 Cals   **1**g Prot   **2**g Fat

Almond Milk
150g Weight   5g Carbs

48 Cals   **5**g Prot   **0**g Fat

Milk (skimmed)
150g Weight   7g Carbs

39 Cals   **4**g Prot   **2**g Fat

Soya Milk (unsweetened)
150g Weight   1g Carbs

69 Cals   **5**g Prot   **3**g Fat

Milk (semi-skimmed)
150g Weight   7g Carbs

65 Cals   **5**g Prot   **4**g Fat

Soya Milk (sweetened)
150g Weight   4g Carbs

99 Cals   **5**g Prot   **6**g Fat

Milk (whole)
150g Weight   7g Carbs

29 Cals **1**g Prot **3**g Fat

Single Cream
15g Weight (tablespoon)   0g Carbs

74 Cals **0**g Prot **8**g Fat

Double Cream
15g Weight (tablespoon)   0g Carbs

88 Cals **0**g Prot **10**g Fat

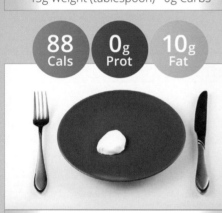

Clotted Cream
15g Weight (tablespoon)   0g Carbs

113 Cals **1**g Prot **12**g Fat

Crème Fraîche
30g Weight (2 tablespoons)   1g Carbs

62 Cals **1**g Prot **6**g Fat

Soured Cream
30g Weight (2 tablespoons)   1g Carbs

112 Cals **1**g Prot **12**g Fat

Whipped Cream
30g Weight (2 tablespoons)   1g Carbs

62 Cals **2**g Prot **5**g Fat

Almonds
10g Weight (tablespoon)   1g Carbs

68 Cals **1**g Prot **7**g Fat

Brazil Nuts
10g Weight (tablespoon)   0g Carbs

61 Cals **2**g Prot **5**g Fat

Cashew Nuts
10g Weight (tablespoon)   2g Carbs

44 Cals **1**g Prot **2**g Fat

Dried Fruit & Nuts
10g Weight   5g Carbs

65 Cals **1**g Prot **6**g Fat

Hazelnuts
10g Weight (tablespoon)   1g Carbs

75 Cals **1**g Prot **8**g Fat

Macadamia
10g Weight   0g Carbs

Peanuts (roasted)

60 Cals **3**g Prot **5**g Fat

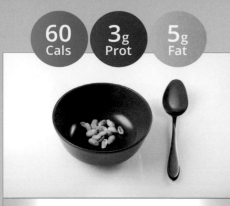

Peanuts *(roasted)*
10g Weight (tablespoon)   1g Carbs

Pecan Nuts

69 Cals **1**g Prot **7**g Fat

Pecan Nuts
10g Weight (tablespoon)   1g Carbs

Pine Nuts

69 Cals **1**g Prot **7**g Fat

Pine Nuts
10g Weight (tablespoon)   0g Carbs

Pistachio

90 Cals **3**g Prot **8**g Fat

Pistachio
30g Weight (with shells)   1g Carbs

Soya Nuts

22 Cals **2**g Prot **1**g Fat

Soya Nuts
6g Weight (tablespoon)   1g Carbs

Walnuts

69 Cals **1**g Prot **7**g Fat

Walnuts
10g Weight (tablespoon)   0g Carbs

50 Cals   **2**g Prot   **4**g Fat

Brown Linseeds
10g Weight (tablespoon)   2g Carbs

53 Cals   **2**g Prot   **4**g Fat

Golden Linseeds
10g Weight (tablespoon)   3g Carbs

57 Cals   **3**g Prot   **5**g Fat

Hemp Seeds
10g Weight (tablespoon)   1g Carbs

57 Cals   **2**g Prot   **5**g Fat

Pumpkin Seeds
10g Weight (tablespoon)   2g Carbs

60 Cals   **2**g Prot   **6**g Fat

Sesame Seeds
10g Weight (tablespoon)   0g Carbs

58 Cals   **2**g Prot   **5**g Fat

Sunflower Seeds
10g Weight (tablespoon)   2g Carbs

49 Cals | **2**g Prot | **0**g Fat

Macaroni
32g Weight   10g Carbs

152 Cals | **5**g Prot | **1**g Fat

Macaroni
100g Weight   30g Carbs

51 Cals | **2**g Prot | **0**g Fat

Pasta Twists
30g Weight   10g Carbs

149 Cals | **5**g Prot | **1**g Fat

Pasta Twists
88g Weight   30g Carbs

50 Cals | **2**g Prot | **0**g Fat

Penne
30g Weight   10g Carbs

150 Cals | **5**g Prot | **1**g Fat

Penne
90g Weight   30g Carbs

71 Cals   **3**g Prot   **2**g Fat

Ravioli *(fresh, meat-filled)*
40g Weight   10g Carbs

203 Cals   **9**g Prot   **5**g Fat

Ravioli *(fresh, meat-filled)*
115g Weight   30g Carbs

52 Cals   **2**g Prot   **0**g Fat

Spaghetti *(white)*
33g Weight   10g Carbs

149 Cals   **5**g Prot   **1**g Fat

Spaghetti *(white)*
95g Weight   30g Carbs

48 Cals   **2**g Prot   **0**g Fat

Spaghetti *(wholemeal)*
33g Weight   10g Carbs

151 Cals   **6**g Prot   **1**g Fat

Spaghetti *(wholemeal)*
105g Weight   30g Carbs

53 Cals   **2**g Prot   **0**g Fat

Tagliatelle
30g Weight   10g Carbs

158 Cals   **5**g Prot   **1**g Fat

Tagliatelle
90g Weight   30g Carbs

114 Cals   **3**g Prot   **2**g Fat

Noodles (egg)
58g Weight   20g Carbs

225 Cals   **6**g Prot   **4**g Fat

Noodles (egg)
115g Weight   40g Carbs

86 Cals   **1**g Prot   **0**g Fat

Noodles (rice)
70g Weight   20g Carbs

175 Cals   **2**g Prot   **0**g Fat

Noodles (rice)
142g Weight   40g Carbs

54 Cals   **1**g Prot   **1**g Fat

Chips *(oven)*
33g Weight   10g Carbs

107 Cals   **2**g Prot   **3**g Fat

Chips *(oven)*
66g Weight   20g Carbs

90 Cals   **3**g Prot   **0**g Fat

Jacket Potato *(with skin)*
95g Weight   20g Carbs

200 Cals   **6**g Prot   **1**g Fat

Jacket Potato *(with skin)*
220g Weight   45g Carbs

82 Cals   **2**g Prot   **0**g Fat

Mashed Potato *(semi-skimmed milk)*
120g Weight   18g Carbs

160 Cals   **5**g Prot   **1**g Fat

Mashed Potato *(semi-skimmed milk)*
235g Weight   36g Carbs

43 Cals   **1**g Prot   **0**g Fat

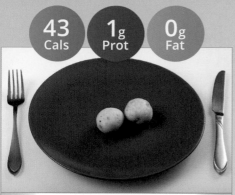

New Potatoes (boiled)
65g Weight   10g Carbs

86 Cals   **2**g Prot   **0**g Fat

New Potatoes (boiled)
130g Weight   20g Carbs

57 Cals   **1**g Prot   **2**g Fat

Roast Potatoes
38g Weight   10g Carbs

142 Cals   **3**g Prot   **4**g Fat

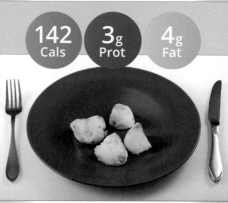

Roast Potatoes
95g Weight   25g Carbs

63 Cals   **1**g Prot   **0**g Fat

Sweet Potatoes (baked)
55g Weight   15g Carbs   ½

124 Cals   **2**g Prot   **0**g Fat

Sweet Potatoes (baked)
108g Weight   30g Carbs   1

89 Cals **2**g Prot **3**g Fat

Wedges *(baked)*
55g Weight   14g Carbs

178 Cals **3**g Prot **6**g Fat

Wedges *(baked)*
110g Weight   28g Carbs

87 Cals **1**g Prot **4**g Fat

Hash Brown *(baked)*
44g Weight   13g Carbs

47 Cals **1**g Prot **3**g Fat

Potato Croquette *(fried)*
22g Weight   5g Carbs

155 Cals **2**g Prot **7**g Fat

Potato Rosti *(grilled)*
80g Weight   20g Carbs

100 Cals **1**g Prot **5**g Fat

Potato Waffle *(baked)*
49g Weight   12g Carbs

46 Cals **1**g Prot **0**g Fat

Basmati Rice
32g Weight   10g Carbs

137 Cals **3**g Prot **1**g Fat

Basmati Rice
96g Weight   30g Carbs

42 Cals **1**g Prot **0**g Fat

Brown Rice *(long grain)*
30g Weight   10g Carbs

134 Cals **3**g Prot **1**g Fat

Brown Rice *(long grain)*
95g Weight   31g Carbs

81 Cals **2**g Prot **1**g Fat

Wild Rice
55g Weight   17g Carbs

252 Cals **5**g Prot **2**g Fat

Wild Rice
170g Weight   52g Carbs

102 Cals **2**g Prot **3**g Fat

Egg Fried Rice
55g Weight   18g Carbs

86 Cals **2**g Prot **1**g Fat

Mexican Rice
55g Weight   17g Carbs

78 Cals **1**g Prot **3**g Fat

Pilau Rice
55g Weight   14g Carbs

88 Cals **3**g Prot **2**g Fat

Rice & Peas
55g Weight   17g Carbs

87 Cals **2**g Prot **2**g Fat

Special Fried Rice
55g Weight   15g Carbs

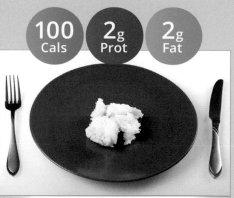

100 Cals **2**g Prot **2**g Fat

Sticky White Rice
70g Weight   19g Carbs

94 Cals   **3**g Prot   **0**g Fat

188 Cals   **5**g Prot   **1**g Fat

Bulgur Wheat
100g Weight   20g Carbs

Bulgur Wheat
200g Weight   40g Carbs

50 Cals   **1**g Prot   **0**g Fat

121 Cals   **3**g Prot   **1**g Fat

Couscous
45g Weight   10g Carbs

Couscous
110g Weight   25g Carbs

109 Cals   **5**g Prot   **2**g Fat

220 Cals   **10**g Prot   **4**g Fat

Quinoa
85g Weight   20g Carbs

Quinoa
172g Weight   40g Carbs

25 Cals **1**g Prot **0**g Fat

Chicken Noodle Soup
130g Weight   4g Carbs

67 Cals **3**g Prot **4**g Fat

Broccoli & Stilton Soup
130g Weight   4g Carbs   ½

28 Cals **1**g Prot **1**g Fat

Miso Soup
200g Weight   2g Carbs

60 Cals **1**g Prot **4**g Fat

Mushroom Soup
130g Weight   5g Carbs   1

81 Cals **1**g Prot **4**g Fat

Tomato Soup
130g Weight   9g Carbs 1

58 Cals **2**g Prot **1**g Fat

Vegetable Soup
130g Weight   11g Carbs   1

37 Cals **0**g Prot **4**g Fat

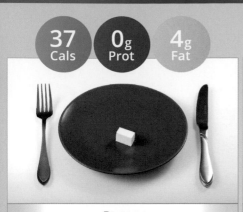

Butter
5g Weight (teaspoon)   0g Carbs

37 Cals **0**g Prot **4**g Fat

Margarine
5g Weight (teaspoon)   0g Carbs

14 Cals **0**g Prot **2**g Fat

Margarine *(light)*
5g Weight (teaspoon)   0g Carbs

36 Cals **0**g Prot **4**g Fat

Olive / Vegetable / Sesame Oil
4g Weight (teaspoon)   0g Carbs

20 Cals **0**g Prot **0**g Fat

Sugar *(white)*
5g Weight (teaspoon)   5g Carbs

2 Cals **0**g Prot **0**g Fat

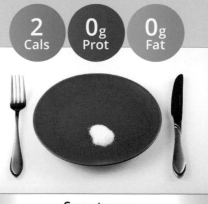

Sweetener
0.5g Weight (teaspoon)   0g Carbs

17 Cals **0**g Prot **0**g Fat

Honey
6g Weight (teaspoon)   5g Carbs

52 Cals **0**g Prot **0**g Fat

Jam
20g Weight (tablespoon)   12g Carbs

45 Cals **0**g Prot **0**g Fat

Maple Syrup
17g Weight (tablespoon)   11g Carbs

52 Cals **0**g Prot **0**g Fat

Marmalade
20g Weight (tablespoon)   14g Carbs

13 Cals **2**g Prot **0**g Fat

Marmite
5g Weight (teaspoon)   1g Carbs

91 Cals **4**g Prot **7**g Fat

Peanut Butter (crunchy)
15g Weight (tablespoon)   2g Carbs

14 Cals **0**g Prot **0**g Fat

BBQ Sauce
15g Weight (tablespoon)   4g Carbs

17 Cals **0**g Prot **0**g Fat

Brown Sauce
17g Weight (tablespoon)   4g Carbs

16 Cals **0**g Prot **0**g Fat

Chilli Sauce
20g Weight (tablespoon)   4g Carbs

30 Cals **0**g Prot **0**g Fat

Cranberry Sauce
20g Weight (tablespoon)   8g Carbs

39 Cals **0**g Prot **3**g Fat

Gravy
115g Weight   4g Carbs

38 Cals **0**g Prot **4**g Fat

Guacamole
30g Weight (2 tablespoons)   1g Carbs

20 Cals **0**g Prot **1**g Fat

Horseradish
13g Weight (tablespoon)   2g Carbs

56 Cals **2**g Prot **4**g Fat

Houmous
30g Weight (2 tablespoons)   3g Carbs

17 Cals **0**g Prot **0**g Fat

Ketchup
15g Weight (tablespoon)   4g Carbs

49 Cals **0**g Prot **0**g Fat

Mango Chutney
20g Weight (tablespoon)   12g Carbs

7 Cals **0**g Prot **0**g Fat

Mustard (English)
5g Weight (teaspoon)   0g Carbs

22 Cals **1**g Prot **2**g Fat

Mustard (wholegrain)
16g Weight (tablespoon)   1g Carbs

43 Cals   **0**g Prot   **4**g Fat

Mayonnaise *(light)*
15g Weight (tablespoon) 1g Carbs

28 Cals   **0**g Prot   **0**g Fat

Pickle
20g Weight (tablespoon) 7g Carbs

52 Cals   **0**g Prot   **5**g Fat

Salad Cream
15g Weight (tablespoon) 3g Carbs

7 Cals   **1**g Prot   **0**g Fat

Soy Sauce
15g Weight (tablespoon) 1g Carbs

33 Cals   **0**g Prot   **0**g Fat

Sweet Chilli Sauce
18g Weight (tablespoon) 8g Carbs

3 Cals   **0**g Prot   **0**g Fat

Worcestershire Sauce
5g Weight (teaspoon) 1g Carbs

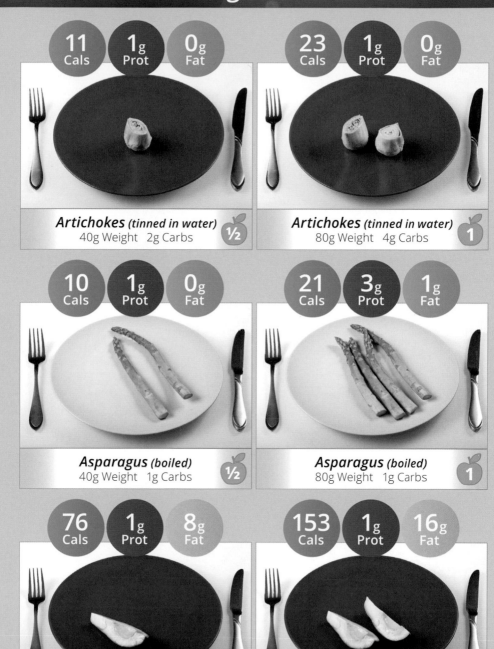

11 Cals **1**g Prot **0**g Fat

Artichokes (tinned in water)
40g Weight 2g Carbs ½

23 Cals **1**g Prot **0**g Fat

Artichokes (tinned in water)
80g Weight 4g Carbs 1

10 Cals **1**g Prot **0**g Fat

Asparagus (boiled)
40g Weight 1g Carbs ½

21 Cals **3**g Prot **1**g Fat

Asparagus (boiled)
80g Weight 1g Carbs 1

76 Cals **1**g Prot **8**g Fat

Avocado
40g Weight 1g Carbs ½

153 Cals **1**g Prot **16**g Fat

Avocado
80g Weight (half) 2g Carbs 1

67 Cals **4g** Prot **0g** Fat

168 Cals **10g** Prot **1g** Fat

Baked Beans in Tomato Sauce
80g Weight   12g Carns **1**

Baked Beans in Tomato Sauce
200g Weight   31g Carbs **1**

3 Cals **0g** Prot **0g** Fat

6 Cals **1g** Prot **0g** Fat

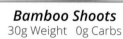

Bamboo Shoots
30g Weight   0g Carbs

Bamboo Shoots
55g Weight   0g Carbs **½**

9 Cals **1g** Prot **0g** Fat

25 Cals **2g** Prot **0g** Fat

Bean Sprouts
30g Weight   1g Carbs

Bean Sprouts
80g Weight   3g Carbs **1**

14 Cals **1**g Prot **0**g Fat

Beetroot *(boiled)*
30g Weight   3g Carbs

37 Cals **2**g Prot **0**g Fat

Beetroot *(boiled)*
80g Weight   8g Carbs

14 Cals **2**g Prot **0**g Fat

Broad Beans *(boiled)*
30g Weight   2g Carbs

26 Cals **3**g Prot **0**g Fat

Broad Beans *(boiled)*
55g Weight   3g Carbs

10 Cals **1**g Prot **0**g Fat

Broccoli *(boiled)*
40g Weight   0g Carbs

19 Cals **3**g Prot **1**g Fat

Broccoli *(boiled)*
80g Weight   1g Carbs

| **31** Cals | **2**g Prot | **0**g Fat | | **62** Cals | **5**g Prot | **0**g Fat |

Butter Beans ½
40g Weight   5g Carbs

Butter Beans 1
80g Weight   10g Carbs

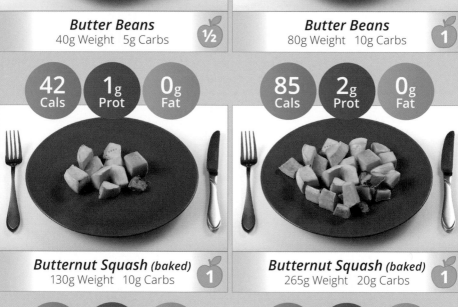

| **42** Cals | **1**g Prot | **0**g Fat | | **85** Cals | **2**g Prot | **0**g Fat |

Butternut Squash *(baked)* 1
130g Weight   10g Carbs

Butternut Squash *(baked)* 1
265g Weight   20g Carbs

| **6** Cals | **0**g Prot | **0**g Fat | | **13** Cals | **1**g Prot | **0**g Fat |

Cabbage *(boiled)* ½
40g Weight   1g Carbs

Cabbage *(boiled)* 1
80g Weight   2g Carbs

10 Cals | **0**g Prot | **0**g Fat

Carrots (boiled) ½
40g Weight   2g Carbs

19 Cals | **1**g Prot | **0**g Fat

Carrots (boiled) 1
80g Weight   4g Carbs

11 Cals | **1**g Prot | **0**g Fat

Cauliflower (boiled) ½
40g Weight   1g Carbs

22 Cals | **2**g Prot | **1**g Fat

Cauliflower (boiled) 1
80g Weight   2g Carbs

3 Cals | **0**g Prot | **0**g Fat

Celery ½
40g Weight   0g Carbs

6 Cals | **0**g Prot | **0**g Fat

Celery 1
80g Weight   1g Carbs

7 Cals **0**g Prot **0**g Fat

Cherry Tomatoes
40g Weight   1g Carbs   ½

14 Cals **1**g Prot **0**g Fat

Cherry Tomatoes
80g Weight   2g Carbs   1

46 Cals **3**g Prot **1**g Fat

Chickpeas
40g Weight   6g Carbs   ½

92 Cals **6**g Prot **2**g Fat

Chickpeas
80g Weight   13g Carbs   1

8 Cals **1**g Prot **0**g Fat

Courgette (boiled)
40g Weight   1g Carbs   ½

15 Cals **2**g Prot **0**g Fat

Courgette (boiled)
80g Weight   2g Carbs   1

4 Cals   **0**g Prot   **0**g Fat

8 Cals   **1**g Prot   **0**g Fat

Cucumber ½
40g Weight   1g Carbs

Cucumber 1
80g Weight   1g Carbs

17 Cals   **2**g Prot   **1**g Fat

33 Cals   **3**g Prot   **1**g Fat

Edamame Beans
55g Weight (30g edible)   1g Carbs

Edamame Beans ½
115g Weight (60g edible)   3g Carbs

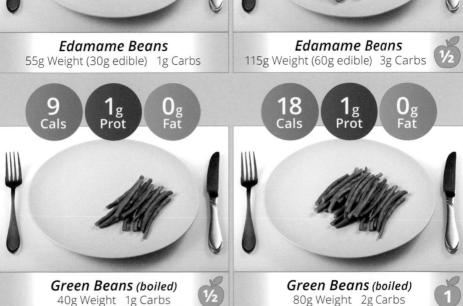

9 Cals   **1**g Prot   **0**g Fat

18 Cals   **1**g Prot   **0**g Fat

Green Beans (boiled) ½
40g Weight   1g Carbs

Green Beans (boiled) 1
80g Weight   2g Carbs

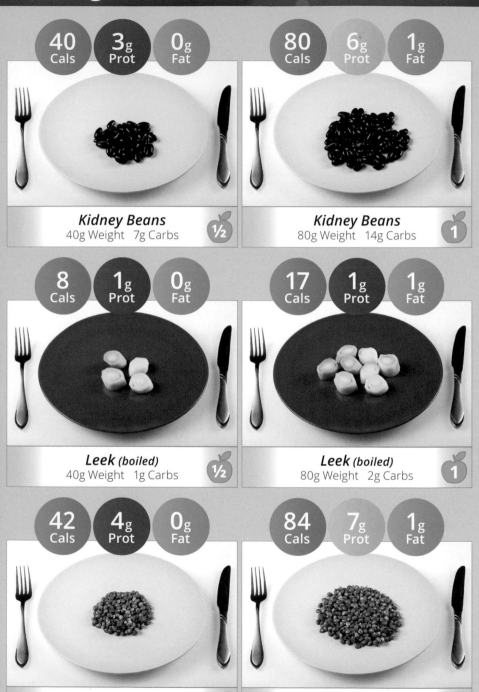

40 Cals **3**g Prot **0**g Fat

Kidney Beans
40g Weight   7g Carbs   ½

80 Cals **6**g Prot **1**g Fat

Kidney Beans
80g Weight   14g Carbs   1

8 Cals **1**g Prot **0**g Fat

Leek (boiled)
40g Weight   1g Carbs   ½

17 Cals **1**g Prot **1**g Fat

Leek (boiled)
80g Weight   2g Carbs   1

42 Cals **4**g Prot **0**g Fat

Lentils (tinned)
40g Weight   7g Carbs   ½

84 Cals **7**g Prot **1**g Fat

Lentils (tinned)
80g Weight   14g Carbs   1

3 Cals **0g** Prot **0g** Fat

Lettuce
25g Weight   1g Carbs

7 Cals **0g** Prot **0g** Fat

Lettuce
50g Weight   1g Carbs   ½

10 Cals **1g** Prot **0g** Fat

Mangetout
40g Weight   1g Carbs   ½

21 Cals **3g** Prot **0g** Fat

Mangetout
80g Weight   3g Carbs   1

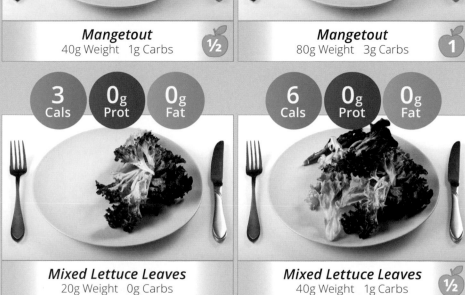

3 Cals **0g** Prot **0g** Fat

Mixed Lettuce Leaves
20g Weight   0g Carbs

6 Cals **0g** Prot **0g** Fat

Mixed Lettuce Leaves
40g Weight   1g Carbs   ½

5 Cals   **1**g Prot   **0**g Fat

10 Cals   **1**g Prot   **0**g Fat

***Mushrooms** (raw)*
40g Weight   0g Carbs   ½

***Mushrooms** (raw)*
80g Weight   0g Carbs   1

11 Cals   **1**g Prot   **0**g Fat

22 Cals   **2**g Prot   **1**g Fat

***Okra** (boiled)*
40g Weight   1g Carbs   ½

***Okra** (boiled)*
80g Weight   2g Carbs   1

14 Cals   **0**g Prot   **0**g Fat

29 Cals   **1**g Prot   **0**g Fat

***Onions** (raw)*
40g Weight   3g Carbs   ½

***Onions** (raw)*
80g Weight   6g Carbs   1

5 Cals   **1**g Prot   **0**g Fat

Pak Choi *(boiled)*
30g Weight   1g Carbs

13 Cals   **1**g Prot   **0**g Fat

Pak Choi *(boiled)*
80g Weight   2g Carbs
1

62 Cals   **1**g Prot   **3**g Fat

Parsnips *(roasted)*
40g Weight   8g Carbs
½

125 Cals   **1**g Prot   **6**g Fat

Parsnips *(roasted)*
80g Weight   15g Carbs
1

28 Cals   **2**g Prot   **0**g Fat

Peas *(boiled)*
40g Weight   4g Carbs
½

55 Cals   **5**g Prot   **1**g Fat

Peas *(boiled)*
80g Weight   8g Carbs
1

6 Cals **0**g Prot **0**g Fat

12 Cals **1**g Prot **0**g Fat

Peppers *(raw)*
40g Weight   1g Carbs   ½

Peppers *(raw)*
80g Weight   2g Carbs   1

65 Cals **5**g Prot **1**g Fat

122 Cals **9**g Prot **1**g Fat

Mushy Peas
80g Weight   11g Carbs   1

Mushy Peas
150g Weight   21g Carbs   1

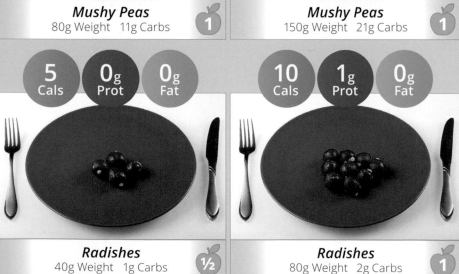

5 Cals **0**g Prot **0**g Fat

10 Cals **1**g Prot **0**g Fat

Radishes
40g Weight   1g Carbs   ½

Radishes
80g Weight   2g Carbs   1

4 Cals **0**g Prot **0**g Fat

Rocket
20g Weight   0g Carbs

8 Cals **1**g Prot **0**g Fat

Rocket
40g Weight   1g Carbs   ½

8 Cals **1**g Prot **0**g Fat

Spinach (boiled)   ½
40g Weight   0g Carbs

15 Cals **2**g Prot **1**g Fat

Spinach (boiled)   1
80g Weight   1g Carbs

8 Cals **1**g Prot **0**g Fat

Spring Greens (boiled)   ½
40g Weight   1g Carbs

16 Cals **2**g Prot **1**g Fat

Spring Greens (boiled)   1
80g Weight   1g Carbs

14 Cals   **1**g Prot   **1**g Fat

28 Cals   **2**g Prot   **1**g Fat

Sprouts (boiled)
40g Weight   1g Carbs   ½

Sprouts (boiled)
80g Weight   3g Carbs   1

49 Cals   **1**g Prot   **0**g Fat

98 Cals   **2**g Prot   **1**g Fat

Sweetcorn
40g Weight   11g Carbs   ½

Sweetcorn
80g Weight   21g Carbs   1

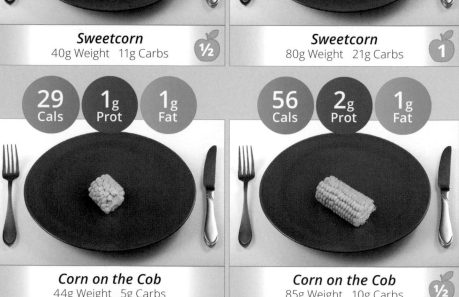

29 Cals   **1**g Prot   **1**g Fat

56 Cals   **2**g Prot   **1**g Fat

Corn on the Cob
44g Weight   5g Carbs

Corn on the Cob
85g Weight   10g Carbs   ½

13 Cals **1**g Prot **0**g Fat

26 Cals **3**g Prot **0**g Fat

Sugar Snap Peas (boiled) ½
40g Weight 2g Carbs

Sugar Snap Peas (boiled) 1
80g Weight 4g Carbs

11 Cals **1**g Prot **0**g Fat

14 Cals **1**g Prot **0**g Fat

Tomato ½
65g Weight 2g Carbs

Tomato 1
80g Weight 3g Carbs

4 Cals **1**g Prot **0**g Fat

9 Cals **1**g Prot **0**g Fat

Watercress
20g Weight 0g Carbs

Watercress ½
40g Weight 0g Carbs

52 Cals   **7**g Prot   **1**g Fat

Quorn Chicken Style Pieces
50g Weight   3g Carbs

85 Cals   **6**g Prot   **7**g Fat

Tofu (fried)
40g Weight   1g Carbs

80 Cals   **7**g Prot   **4**g Fat

Quorn Burger (grilled)
38g Weight   4g Carbs

228 Cals   **5**g Prot   **10**g Fat

Vegetarian Burger (grilled)
100g Weight   28g Carbs

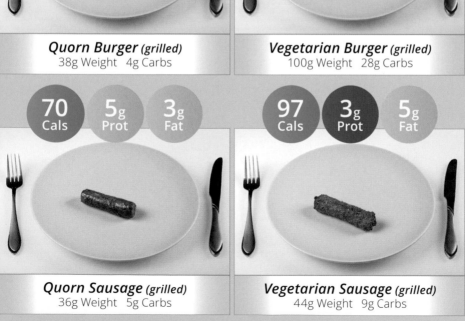

70 Cals   **5**g Prot   **3**g Fat

Quorn Sausage (grilled)
36g Weight   5g Carbs

97 Cals   **3**g Prot   **5**g Fat

Vegetarian Sausage (grilled)
44g Weight   9g Carbs

131 Cals   **5**g Prot   **4**g Fat

Fruit Yogurt
125g Weight   17g Carbs

72 Cals   **6**g Prot   **0**g Fat

Fruit Yogurt (fat-free)
125g Weight   11g Carbs

96 Cals   **9**g Prot   **3**g Fat

Greek Yogurt (low-fat)
125g Weight   8g Carbs

91 Cals   **3**g Prot   **2**g Fat

Soya Yogurt
125g Weight   16g Carbs

99 Cals   **7**g Prot   **4**g Fat

Natural Yogurt
125g Weight   10g Carbs

70 Cals   **6**g Prot   **1**g Fat

Natural Yogurt (low-fat)
125g Weight   9g Carbs

Recipe & Snack Index

Individual Food Index

About the authors

Chris Cheyette BSc (Hons) MSc RD
Diabetes Specialist Dietitian

Chris is a Diabetes Specialist Dietitian within the NHS, working with people with Type 1, Type 2 and gestational diabetes. Chris has spearheaded a number of projects over the years, many with the aim of improving diabetes educational resources. These include an educational DVD for young people with diabetes, which earned him the 2007 British Dietetic Association Elizabeth Washington Award. Chris has also published a number of journal articles on weight management and diabetes. He regularly undertakes local and national presentations to healthcare professionals, has done TV & newspaper interviews, and has participated as a guest expert in online discussions.

Yello Balolia BA (Hons)
Entrepreneur & Creative Photographer

Having achieved a first class honours degree in Photography, Canada-born Blackpool-bred and now London-based Yello used his entrepreneurial and creative skills to found Chello Publishing Limited with Chris Cheyette, to publish Carbs & Cals (www.carbsandcals.com), the bestselling and multi-award-winning book and app for diabetes and weight management. He has also undertaken a series of creative projects including private commissions (www.yellobalolia.com) and, as a keen musician, Yello recently set up Ukulology - a visual and effective way of learning the ukulele (www.ukulology.com).

Awards

Carbs & Cals won **Best Dietary Management Initiative** at the Quality in Care Awards 2014

The *Carbs & Cals App* won **New Product of the Year** in the Complete Nutrition Awards 2012

Carbs & Cals won the BDA Dame Barbara Clayton **Award for Innovation & Excellence** 2011